THE
SCANDINAVIAN
HERITAGE

THE
SCANDINAVIAN
HERITAGE

Arland O. Fiske

North American Heritage Press
Minot, North Dakota

THE SCANDINAVIAN HERITAGE

Copyright © **1987**
by Arland O. Fiske

International Standard Book Number: 0-942323-00-9

Library of Congress Catalog Number: 87-60604

Cover design by
Sheldon Larson of Creative Media, Minot, ND.

Cover photo by
Reimann Photography, Minot, ND.

Fourth Printing, 1989

Published by
North American Heritage Press
A DIVISION OF
CREATIVE MEDIA, INC.
P.O. Box 1
Minot, North Dakota 58702
701/852-5552

Printed in the United States of America

Dedication

To Gerda—
my Danish-American wife
of 35 years.

CONTENTS

THE SCANDINAVIAN HERITAGE

x

FOREWORD

ARLAND FISKE IS A GOOD STORY TELLER. In these vignettes he has taken events in Scandinavian history and made them live and breathe. Some of them deal with well-known historical figures; others tell us of persons and places that do not dominate the pages of history. But there is a human warmth and interest in each one.

There is a kind of ethnic glorification that takes place as we re-tell the stories of our heritage. We can be led to believe that our forebearers in those lands of northern Europe were almost super-human.

On the other hand there is also the danger that we forget the past and those whose footprints mark its sands. There is little virtue in turning our backs on the record of people struggling, enjoying life, setting out on adventures and making lasting contributions to human-kind.

So a collection such as Fiske presents serves us well. It helps us remember some of the worthwhile things about the Scandinavians of a distant and a not-so-distant past.

One virtue of this collection of articles is its breadth. So often we read about the Norwegians or the Swedes or the Danes or the Finns, they are presented almost as competitors for places in history. Here is an author who is attracted to and charmed by the exploits and accomplishments of all the Scandinavians. The reader may make comparisons or draw contrasts; the author does not.

Fiske's collection of "little stories" is easily read and can be taken a bit at a time if preferred. Each story has its own attraction.

There is no doubt an almost endless supply of material for sketches such as these. We can no doubt look forward to more of them as we enjoy the ones presented here.

—Dr. Sidney A. Rand
Former President of St. Olaf College
and United States Ambassador to Norway

PREFACE

IN 1977, MY WIFE AND I, together with five of our seven children, travelled in Denmark and Norway for a month. It was the 25th anniversary for our marriage and for my ordination. In the early 1980s, I started to write some stories about Scandinavian heritage for our family, as they were scattered in various parts of the United States. In March 1983, my good friend Allen O. Larson started a weekly newspaper called the "Area Market Review," which had about a 40,000 circulation in north central North Dakota. Knowing of these stories written for my family, he asked if I might submit a few for his new publishing venture. I agreed and thought that perhaps about 10 would be publishable. Almost four years later, nearly 200 stories have appeared, both to my delight and surprise. This volume contains the first 100 stories published.

The stories are of many kinds. Some reflect ancient history and folklore, others are about modern Scandinavians and Scandinavian-Americans who have brought pride to their heritage, and some are just folksy stories about the things that have been a lot of fun for our family in the pursuit of the Scandinavian heritage.

They appear in the order in which they were printed in the "Area Market Review," but have been changed where necessary for publishing in a book. Chapters 37-100 are shorter than the earlier ones due to the limitations for space in the weekly paper.

My interest in publishing these stories is to offer a basis for pride in heritage. While I have tried to do careful research on the stories, I do not claim to be a Scandinavian historian, but rather a storyteller and popularizer of the tradition. Even though our children and grandchildren were the original group for whom they were intended, the public response to these stories indicates that many more people have found them to be interesting. Some people have clipped them out of the newspapers to keep in a scrapbook and others have mailed them to friends all over the world. Needless to say, I'm pleased that there should be so much interest in them.

My wife, Gerda, whose family came from Denmark, has given me invaluable assistance by listening to the stories read aloud, as well as reading the manuscripts, before they were submitted to print. She lets me know when something doesn't sound right. Sometimes our children have offered their critique before the weekly publication. I'm grateful for their interest in the heritage which we share and cherish.

If it seems that the stories are tilted a bit to the Norwegian side of the heritage, this is not because I lack appreciation for other Scandinavians, but because I grew up in the Red River Valley of North Dakota, which was a "Norwegian America." These are the people I knew best as a child. The language was still spoken and many of the immigrants were still alive. I cannot claim to be "Norwegian" as my cousins in the "Old World" are, but rather a "Norwegian-American" who loves both America and the lands of Scandinavia. I hope that people of other nationalities can also enjoy these stories. There are a lot of wonderful people in this "New World" and it's important that we share the best of our heritages with each other. It builds better communities.

Mention needs to be made of the Norsk Høstfest, founded in 1978 in Minot. This annual event has encouraged many of us to share our pride in heritage. The publication of the first edition of the "Scandinavian Heritage Calendar" in 1983 has also furthered the research that found its way into these stories.

My special thanks go to Allen O. Larson and his North American Heritage Press for encouragement to publish these stories, to Tammy Wolf for preparing the manuscript for publication, to my daughter, Lisa Gaylor, for drawing the illustrations and to Sheldon Larson for the cover design. Thanks to the many people who have shown interest in the "Scandinavian Heritage Column." Happy reading!

—Arland O. Fiske
  Minot, North Dakota
  New Year's Day 1987

CHAPTER 1

Who Are
The Scandinavians?

THE PEOPLE OF FIVE NATIONS make up the Scandinavian heritage. These are: Denmark, Finland, Iceland, Norway and Sweden. The Scandinavians, however, have been a travelling people and now live in all parts of the world. Their greatest concentration is found in the USA with large numbers in the upper Midwest states and on the West Coast.

The Scandinavian lands, with the exception of Iceland, are known to have been inhabited since before the last Ice Age. People have lived in Denmark since about 10,000 B.C. and in Norway, Sweden and Finland since 7000-8000 B.C. Iceland was not settled until the ninth century A.D., though Irish monks had arrived two centuries earlier. Iceland was settled by Norwegians fleeing from the tyranny of King Harald Haarfagre (Finehair). The Icelandic people of today still speak the Old Norse of that period. The Danes, Norwegians and Swedes are a distinct Teutonic language group and share a common heritage with the North Germans and Dutch. This Germanic immigration to the Scandinavian lands began about 2000 B.C. and covered a lengthy period of time.

There are, of course, no pure races. In addition to the typically blonde and blue eyed Scandinavians, there are many with darker complexion that settled especially in western Norway. Many flaxen haired Celts were taken as slaves from Ireland and blended in with the Norwegians. They were given their freedom after Norway became Christian.

The term Scandinavia was originally Scatinavia, and was a misspelling in the writings of Pliny the Elder. In 5 A.D., Emperor Augustus sent his Rhine fleet to explore the region and then it became forgotten from the pages of history for almost 400 years.

The people of Finland are a part of a migration that passed through Hungary and Estonia. Because Finland was under Swedish rule from 1216 to 1809, there are many Finns of Swedish origin especially in the southwestern part of the country, around Turku, the old Swedish

1

capital. Swedish is an official language of Finland today, together with Finnish. In 1809, Russia occupied Finland and it did not gain its independence until 1917. The Russians made Finland a Grand Duchy and chose Helsinki for their capital. This was closer to St. Petersburg (now Leningrad), the home of the Czars.

During the ninth through the eleventh centuries, the Germanic Scandinavians spread out in a series of conquests and colonizations to England, Scotland, Ireland, the North Sea islands, Russia and the Baltic areas. They carried on trade in a much larger area and were given possession of that part of France called Normandy (Northmandy). If you find some French people with blonde hair and blue eyes, ask if they are Normans.

But where have all the Vikings gone? Are they only in the movies and comic strips? And what kind of people were they really like? These hardy people who knew no fear in war or on the high seas, whose cruelty earned them a fearsome reputation, became eager settlers in the lands where they waged war. Once they became colonists, they became traders instead of raiders. They also became peaceful patriots, often joining in defensive wars against their former countrymen. Though war was a part of their culture, their main interests were trading and finding places to live for the people of their overcrowded homelands. Primogeniture was the law of the land. This meant that only the oldest son was entitled to inherit the family farm and other property. He also had to care for his parents for so long as they lived.

In America, the Scandinavian immigrants became fiercely patriotic to the cause of the New World. They were a willing part of the melting pot. My parents would not speak a word of Norwegian to me. That was left to one of my grandmothers who refused to speak a word of English to anyone. Education was of highest priority to these immigrants. Parents would sacrifice all luxuries and conveniences so that their children could get a high school diploma and a college degree. They also established many fine colleges which are still flourishing. The result was that a high proportion of the Scandinavian immigrant families became leaders in politics, science, education, the church and in the arts.

Scandinavianism as a modern movement began after the fall from greatness of the two powers, Denmark and Sweden, early in the 19th century. Students led the way. Meeting in Copenhagen, they pledged to be true to each other "in life and in death in their loyalty to our great common fatherland." Since the super powers of the day feared the political rise of a Scandinavian kingdom, the alliance was kept in the bounds of culture and trade. There was also a strong nationalism in each country which wanted to support the special interests of each nation.

Peace, not war, is the trademark of the Scandinavians today. This is evident in the fact that the first two Secretary Generals of the United Nations came from Scandinavia: Trygve Lie of Norway and Dag Hamarskjold of Sweden.

Small countries need good memories. The people of Scandinavia have learned well how to live as close neighbors to the Warsaw Pact nations and still preserve their heritage of freedom. It was a long time dream of my family to visit Scandinavia. It was quite a surprise to our children to learn that it was the dream of Scandinavian children to go to America. Without doubt, they are some of the best friends America has in the world. Long live the lands of the Northmen and their children everywhere!

CHAPTER 2

General L. J. Sverdrup— "Engineer Soldier At His Best"

"ENGINEER SOLDIER AT HIS BEST," this is how General Douglas MacArthur described the son of a Lutheran parsonage who immigrated to America from Norway at age 16. Leif Johan Sverdrup is possibly the most honored Norwegian to have lived in the New World.

How did this immigrant boy from the west coast of Norway attain to such fame? He arrived in America on Dec. 7, 1914, sponsored by a relative, Jorgen Heiberg, of Twin Valley, Minnesota. To begin with, he worked on farms in the area and even taught "parochial" (religious) school. At age 18, he entered Augsburg College in Minneapolis and earned a bachelor of arts degree in two years. After serving in the U.S. Army in World War I, he earned another degree, this time in engineering at the University of Minnesota. His first job was with the Missouri State Highway Department where he proved his ability that was later to become so famous. It was not long before his engineering professor, John Ira Parcel, joined him in forming Sverdrup & Parcel and Associates, Inc. which became one of the world's largest and most respected engineering and architectural firms. The headquarters are in St. Louis.

By the time of World War II, Sverdrup had become world famous. In August 1941, the State Department asked him to build a chain of airstrips in the Philippines which could land B-17s. MacArthur expected a Japanese attack by April 1942, when the monsoon season was over. When Sverdrup delayed his answer, he was told, "You gotta do it." He went and did a job which still defies belief.

Sverdrup never did get to the Philippines on that trip. The Japanese arrived first. But he did build a chain of airfields that moved the U.S. planes to victory up through the South Sea islands. One of the most interesting stories told of his many exploits was how he got the runways packed hard enough to land the big planes. According to the St. Louis Post-Dispatch, "He would send his native interpreter ahead to a new

4

village to announce that a supernatural man was coming. Then Sverdrup would march in carrying his wind-up phonograph. The awed natives built his airfields by day and were rewarded with dances at night. Shortly after the last pair of dancing feet had padded down the new airfield and had gone home to rest, the airplanes would come roaring in."

Sverdrup built more than 200 airfields and related military projects. It is no wonder that General MacArthur stated on Jan. 12, 1945, on a heavy cruiser in Lingayen Gulf: "This is the engineer soldier at his best."

After the war, Sverdrup continued his energies for peace as a devoted family man and to rebuild downtown St. Louis. He had a great deal to do with developing the city's famous riverfront which includes the Arch and the Busch Memorial Stadium. The Boy Scouts of America awarded him their highest honor, the Silver Buffalo. By this time, he had become a personal friend of presidents and kings.

On a trip to the nation's capital, he noted that there was no statue of St. Olaf in the Washington Cathedral. The Sverdrups commissioned a sculptor and presented a memorial to Norway's patron saint.

I had not lived long in St. Louis, having arrived in late 1961, when people began to tell me about the famous Norwegian who had become a legend in their city. The Sverdrups, of course, had already distinguished themselves as one of Norway's best known families. They were leaders in government, church, Arctic exploration and scientific research. They had come to America too: Both an uncle and a cousin of Leif had been presidents of Augsburg College and Seminary. He never lost his love for Norway, serving as the Norwegian Vice Counsul in St. Louis. He was known to say that the "shortest distance between two points was through Norway." He returned often.

My first appointment with this famous Norseman was on Oct. 1, 1962. I asked his support to promote a concert by the St. Olaf Choir the following February. I was not disappointed. He made me feel at ease with his natural friendliness. He offered his help and with one phone call to his friend, Richard Amberg, Editor of the St. Louis Globe-Democrat, I had a story in the newspaper.

We met several more times, once in our home. At his funeral on

5

Jan. 5, 1976, messages were read from President Ford and King Olav V. It was fitting that at such a service the congregation should sing, "A Mighty Fortress is our God!" MacArthur was right! And his legend lives on.

CHAPTER 3

Queen Margaret I—
Ruler Of All Scandinavia

"GOD BE PRAISED TO ALL ETERNITY that he laid this unexpected victory in the hands of a woman, put shackles on the feet of kings and handcuffs on their nobles." This is how a Danish chronicler expressed the feelings of many after the Battle of Asla, Sweden, in 1389, when Margaret became the supreme ruler of the Scandinavian lands. From Lake Ladoga in Finland to Greenland in the west, and from North Cape in the far north of Norway to the Eider River on the south, this emancipated woman ruled with shrewdness, charm, patience, self-confidence, religious faith and an aura of integrity.

Who was this woman of such ability and how did she attain her great power? Margaret was born in 1346, the daughter of Danish king Valdemar IV. It was not a good time. The "Black Death" had travelled across Europe when she was but a little girl. In 1349, it came to Denmark, Norway and Sweden, all in one year. Two thirds of Norway's population, one third of Denmark's and as many in Sweden died in swift order. It brought out the worst in people. Death was dealt to those accused of "poisoning" the wells. Jews were especially marked out for pogrom. Disease, starvation and poverty reduced the ability of the north lands to govern themselves. Many villages were decimated and the land reverted to forests and the wild animals. Death spread particularly among the clergy, as they were required to minister to the dying.

It was into this world of realism that Margaret was bargained off in marriage through a treaty between the kings of Norway and Denmark. At age 10, she was hustled off to Akershus, the fortress castle in the Oslo harbor. For six years she did not live with her husband, King Haakon VI, while he was busy leading armies and seeking fame. She was treated more as a helpless royal hostage in those early years, rather than as a Danish princess or the Queen of Norway.

Times were hard in the royal palace too. She and her household were in danger of starvation, not to mention freezing to death in that old fortress. Margaret had to write to her husband begging for money. "I have to inform you, my dear lord, that I and my servants suffer dire need of food and drink, such that neither I or they get the necessities." We don't know if she received the money or not. But Margaret had two things going for her. First, she had inherited her father's strong will and second, her governess was the daughter of one of the most famous women in Swedish history, "St. Birgitta." Birgitta is still revered for her piety, courage and visions, which often had a political inference.

When Margaret was 17, she gave birth to a son, Olaf. He was only five when his grandfather, King Valdemar of Denmark, died. Olaf was elected king of Denmark, but Margaret served as regent. Just five years later in 1380, his father died. The boy king was recognized as Olaf IV of Norway and ruled with his mother as advisor. At this time Slesvig was added to Denmark and much of Sweden also fell in line. The young Olaf died in 1387 at just 17 years of age. With him, came the end of the male line of Norse kings which had begun with Harald Haarfagre ("Finehair") and included Olaf Trygvasson and Olaf Haraldsson (St. Olaf). The new ruling family traced its line to Gorm, the founder of the present royal Danish house.

Margaret knew how to handle the situation. She used her influence to have her sister's grandson, three year old Eric of Pomerania, elected king. He was also the nephew of Sweden's King Albert. Though Eric was crowned king of all Scandinavia in 1397 at age 13, Margaret remained the real ruler until her death in 1412.

The rule of this strong woman was agreed to by both the nobles and the bishops. In Denmark, she was called the "all powerful lady and mistress and the regent of the whole Danish kingdom." The crowning event of Margaret's political skill was the Union of Kalmar signed on July 13, 1397, which bound the Scandinavian countries into one kingdom. It was written that they "should eternally have one king and not several so that the realms will never again be divided, if God wills."

How did this little girl, who was bargained off into a marriage designed as a part of a political treaty, become the mightiest ruler of the North Sea? There are many factors including accidents of birth and death, pressure by the merchants of the Hanseatic League and other rivals destroying each other. But it was mostly Margaret herself, her personal charm and her belief that she was born to rule.

Margaret is a proud name in Scandinavia. Now I understand the confident look on the picture of my great grandmother in Surnadal who bore that name. Long live Margaret I and Margaret II, who is the present Queen of Denmark.

Margrethe Jonsdotter Røv Fiske.

CHAPTER 4

April 9, 1940—
The "Bitter Years" Begin

IT WAS A FEW MINUTES BEFORE 5 A.M. on April 9, 1940. This was the day the Nazi war machine unleashed "Weseruebung," its attack on Denmark and Norway. In Copenhagen, invasion combat forces silently disembarked from the troopship "Hansestadt Danzig" and swarmed into the Citadel, the central military headquarters.

The attacks were planned to strike key places simultaneously in the two Scandinavian lands. In Denmark, Jutland and Fyn were also occupied with only token resistance. Pro-Nazi Danish citizens even directed traffic for the invaders. Some wore swastikas and shouted "Heil Hitler."

The targets in Norway were Narvik, Trondheim, Stavanger, Bergen, Kristiansand and Oslo. The attacks began before dawn and the occupation was completed by midday except in Kristiansand and Oslo. In Trondheim, Knut Lovseth woke up early and heard strange voices from his lawn. The voices spoke German. At his father's urging, he fled to the mountains.

Christian X, King of Denmark, openly scorned the warning that his country was in danger. On the evening of April 8th, the king was advised that Denmark might be invaded. He replied that he couldn't "really believe that" and then went off to the theatre to watch a performance of "The Merry Wives of Windsor." All day long on April 9th, people in Bindslev, a town near the North Sea, listened to the roar of airplanes travelling northward. "Poor Norway," they said.

In Norway, Christian's brother, Haakon VII, refused the enemy's ultimatum to surrender. He stalled the Nazi negotiators for a time, while fighting rear guard action along the mountain roads. Carl J. Hambro, President of the Storting (Parliament), was tireless in his energies to protect the king's life and freedom. Crown Prince Olav was with the king, while the royal family fled to Sweden. But patriotism alone was no match for the Luftwaffe and invading paratroopers. Destruction was ruthless wherever there was resistance.

British, French and Polish troops entered the war in Norway. The biggest battle was at Narvik. This northern seaport city was essential to the Nazi war effort as it handled shipments of iron ore brought from Sweden by train. Here the Allies gave Hitler his first defeat on May 28. But just six days later, the evacuation order was given. The Blitzkrieg had been hurled against the Lowlands and France on May 10. The eyes of the world were breathlessly watching Dunkirk. Churchill ordered the Allied troops to leave Norway and to defend England. King Haakon, seeing the futility of further struggle, departed for London on the cruiser "Devonshire."

Why had the invasion succeeded so brilliantly? Totalitarian governments always have the initial advantage in war. They are not strapped with a free press or the need for parliamentary debates. Surprise is on their side. Perhaps the weather was the chief factor. The invasion fleet escaped the detection of the British Navy. Still the invaders paid a price that Churchill claimed affected the final outcome of the war. When the brief but bitter battle for Norway was over, almost the entire Nazi Navy had been destroyed.

In Oslo, Vikdun Quisling set up a new government. He was determined to gain favor with authorities in Berlin. In Denmark, Hitler hoped to create a model state for his "New Order." He needed its agricultural products. The Danish Nazi party made an attempt to assert itself through elections but was soundly rejected.

In Washington, the Danish Ambassador, Henrik Kauffmann, severed all ties with the government in Copenhagen and declared himself a representative of "Free Denmark." He made a treaty which placed Greenland under American protection.

Organized resistance arose in both countries. Great acts of heroism are recorded together with tragic deaths. The British flew in drops of guns, two way radios, dynamite and saboteurs. It was not, however, until 1943 that hostilities reached open rebellion in Denmark. On August 29, the Nazi's admitted their failure to convert the Danes to Hitler's "New Order" and they put a clamp of iron over the land.

Massive arrest of Denmark's 8000 Jews was ordered. Less than 500

were imprisoned. The rest fled to Sweden, sometimes with the cooperation of German officers who looked the other way. Sweden tried to
maintain neutrality throughout the war and was highly criticized by
many. But in October 1943, they defied Hitler and won the respect of
the Allied powers.

After 126 years of peace in Norway and 76 in Denmark, the bitter
years began. Darkness shaded their faces for over five years. When the
war was over, the people of Denmark tore off the thick shades and lit
candles in their windows, just as they do at Christmas. Freedom is,
afterall, the greatest gift which can belong to any people.

CHAPTER 5

"Prillar-Guri:" The Country Girl Who Saved Norway

PERHAPS YOU HAVE SEEN a picture of a Norwegian girl play-ing a long horn called a "lur." If so, it was likely meant to be "Prillar-Guri." It's a story that inspires courage and patriotism. The year was 1612. There was war between the joint kingdom of Denmark-Norway and Sweden. In those days, there were often disputes between the Scandinavian powers that led to military conflicts.

The political decisions for the joint kingdom were made in Copen-hagen. King Christian IV was the leader of a kingdom joined by the "Union of Kalmar" in 1397, when Margaret I was queen. In this war, the Swedish King had recruited mercenaries from Holland and Scotland to come to his aid.

It has happened only a few times in history that the "savior" of a na-tion has been a woman, and hardly ever a girl of 17. Guri was an ex-ception. She played a key role in defending the land. For over 350 years, the story of "Prillar-Guri" had been told, but no book could be found on it. In 1968, Arthur Stavig went to Norway to look for the complete story. After a painstaking search, he discovered it was being serialized in the *Romsdal Budstikke*, a daily newspaper. He took the story back to America and together with Marvel Arseth DeSordi translated it in-to English. Now the whole world can read about this heroine of old Norway.

Guri was an orphan and had been reared by foster parents in Roms-dalen, near Molde. She had been a sickly girl and for this reason was taken to an old stave church up in the File Mountains (Filefjell) for prayers of healing. St. Thomas Church was the place for pilgrims to visit on Annunciation Day (March 25). Many of them left their crutches behind as they journeyed home. Whether it was the prayers, the long hike in the mountain air or a combination of both, we do not know, but Guri became radiantly healthy. She was getting ready for her wed-ding to Kjell, just as soon as he returned from the war. Little did they suspect that their lives would be tragically changed by an event already

13

in progress of which they were innocent. Invading mercenaries would pass directly through their valley.

The Scots might have travelled through to Sweden with little incident, as did the Dutch through Trondheim, if their leader, Col. George Sinclair, had not decided on a campaign of terror to conquer Norway first. Sinclair was a soldier with a charisma for leadership but whose ambition would not hesitate to employ the vilest treachery. His army, with two notable exceptions, was a band of cut-throats, recruited from the lowest dregs of society in western Europe. Their arrival on August 10 began a 16-day reign of terror which has not been forgotten. Every farm building was burned to the ground, children and old people murdered and maidens were ravished. They looted and feasted on whatever food and liquor they could find. To make it even more frightful, Sinclair had a huge bloodhound named "Ralf" that was able to sniff out people and farms at a great distance.

Because of the war with Sweden, there were only old men with crude weapons to defend the valley which led to Gudbrandsdal, Kjell's home. Beyond that lay the unguarded heartland of central Norway. It was Guri, the seter girl, who carried the warning to the unsuspecting farmlands. She travelled through streams and underbrush, hiding from Sinclair and his dog. He had seen her and had resolved to make her his prize of war. She travelled without regard to pain and danger of the wild animals in the mountains. With every breath, she prayed, "Lord Jesus, lead me to warn the people and to save Kjell's family from this terrible enemy". When she arrived at the end of her journey, she didn't look much like a bride. But the people had been warned and now worked feverishly to build an ambush at a narrow pass near Kringen, upstream from Lesje and Dovre.

In the strangest of happenings, Mary Sinclair was also hurrying through the mountains, trying to stop her husband. Carrying her new born son, she wept bitter tears at her husband's deeds.

An avalanche of rocks was constructed to greet the invaders. Just beyond a bend on a narrow pass, a barricade was built. Across the river in plain sight of the enemy stood Guri. She was dressed in her bridal clothes, her wedding with Kjell having just been completed, as he had unexpectedly returned from the war. Guri played her lur as a signal to the defenders that the hated enemy was approaching.

A musket shot from the bushes mortally wounded Sinclair. Then the rocks began to roll. Almost all of the 800 invaders perished. Of the survivors, only 16 escaped massacre by the angry farmers.

The victory for Norway brought a tragic end to Guri's dreams. In the aftermath of the mellee, Kjell tried to save Sinclair's son from harm. The child's mother, overcome with grief and fearing for her son, misunderstood Kjell's intentions and stabbed him to death. Guri's marriage lasted only hours, but she is remembered for what took place at Kringen that day, Aug. 26, 1612. "Prillar-Guri" will live forever as a national hero in Norway's long struggle for freedom.

CHAPTER 6

The Vikings
In Ireland

"Bitter is the wind tonight,
  White the tresses of the sea;
I have no fear the Viking hordes
  Will sail the sea on such a night."

THIS IS HOW AN IRISH MONK described the feelings of St. Patrick's land in the ninth century. Stormy seas meant protection from Norwegian and Danish invasions. Calm seas sent fear into everyone's hearts.

The Norwegian Vikings were the first to reach the green fields and heather of Ireland with a raid in A.D. 617. It was brutal, in the style of the times. Then followed 150 years of peace and friendly trade. But as the stories of this fair land were told during the long and cold, wintry nights of Norway's dark valleys, future invasions were conceived.

The "Viking Age" in Ireland began with a series of raids beginning in 795 near a place called "Dubh-Linn" (black pool). There the Vikings built a city about 837 to shelter their longships. Today it is called Dublin. It became the center of the earliest Norse kingdom, even before Norway itself was united under one rule. For 300 years, Scandinavians were an everyday part of Irish life. Before the era had ended, Ireland was transformed from a pastoral society built around monasteries into a land of cities and trade with minted coins. Even the name "Ireland" comes from the Norse "Ira-land." Many places such as Wexford, Waterford, Arklow and Wicklow have Norse origins.

Why did the Scandinavians come to Ireland? There are two main reasons. First, they needed room for expansion. The laws of inheritance gave the farm to the oldest son. Even today only about 4% of Norway's land is agriculturally useful. The landless sons and those desiring adventure looked to the sea and foreign lands for opportunity, just as later they looked to America. Second, piracy was not considered a dishonorable profession in those days. When the Vikings discovered that the

16

monasteries served as the "banks" to safeguard people's jewels and precious metals, it was an easy matter for sea-hardened warriors to plunder this wealth. Many articles "made in Ireland" have been found buried in the cemeteries of Denmark and Norway. Norsemen brought much of the loot back to their wives who proudly displayed their husband's successes at sea.

The Irish referred to the Norwegians as "White Gentiles" (heathen) because they wore leather tunics in battle. The Danes were called "Black Gentiles" because they wore dark colored armor. The Danes preferred battle axes as weapons, while the Norwegians were partial to swords.

As often happens in war, many Irish collaborated with the enemy. A mixed race developed from intermarriage and the adoption of Irish children by the invaders. They were called "foreign Irish" and became notorious cattle thieves and soldiers for hire.

The Ireland into which these fierce Northmen came was an outstanding society of saints, scholars and kings. It is one of the ironies of history that the vanquished often have higher civilizations than the victors. It is not stretching the truth to claim that Ireland was the most Christian land of the Middle Ages. What made the Viking invasions so frightful in their early years was the attempt to establish the gods of Germanic paganism, Odin, Thor and Frey, with its system of human sacrifice. The Irish were not without tribal wars or other faults, but they were a model civilization amidst the barbarity of the times.

As the Norsemen settled down, they often fought alongside the Irish in resisting later Viking invasions. It is also true that many Irish were allies of the invaders. The Vikings, in time, became Christian and Dublin became a center of churches. Foreign mission work reached out to England, which had become paganized through Anglo-Saxon invasions from northwest Germany and Denmark. This ultimately led to the conversion of Norway itself by way of England. The flaxen-haired Celtic people of Ireland and the blonde and red-haired Scandinavians together have become the Irish of today.

There came a day, however, when the two cultures clashed in a decisive battle. It was near Dublin at the seaside city of Clontarf. Sigtrygg ("silkbeard"), the Norse king of Dublin, amassed 20,000 soldiers from many lands in the North Sea. He was matched by an equal number of Irish and Scandinavian allies. The Irish leader was the saintly and popular Brian Boru, the son of a chieftain named Kennedy. Brian, a devout Christian, was 73 years old but still a strong man. It was Holy Week and troops began to form lines on Palm Sunday. Brian did not want to do battle on Good Friday. The Vikings, fully aware of this, attacked. Brian, being faithful to his religious convictions, spent the day in prayer, guarded by a ring of shields. The Norsemen were better armed but had poorer field position. At the end of that day, April 23, 1014, Brian had won a crushing victory. But it was also a day of tragedy for Ireland. Brian and his sons, who had the ability to give stable leadership to Ireland's future, were all killed. As Brian knelt in prayer, a Viking warrior broke through the guard and struck him down. Ironically, the berserk Norseman had been prodded to the deed by an ambitious, charming but vengeful woman whom Brian had spurned in marriage.

Many Scandinavians settled in Ireland to become wealthy merchants and "Irish." Don't be surprised when you meet people who are proud to be Irish but have names that betray Norse origins.

A surprise ending to this story appeared in the *Chicago Tribune*, Nov. 11, 1980. Research on President Ronald Reagan's ancestry produced this report: "Reagan is descended from Brian Boru, an 11th century high king of all Ireland and the Emerald Isle's first national hero."

CHAPTER 7

The Scandinavian "Oscars"
And The "French Connection"

EVERYONE KNOWS THAT AN "OSCAR" is an award for outstanding acting in the movies. Long before there was a Holly-
wood, two "Oscars" were kings of Sweden: Oscar I (1844-1859)
and Oscar II (1872-1907). Actually, the Oscars of Sweden were
not Swedes at all, but French. The stage for this change in Scandinavian politics came through the wars of Napoleon.

Denmark and Norway had shared the same rulers since Queen
Margaret I in 1380, when the last "Norwegian" king of Norway died.
The arrangement seemed eternal. This was made clear to me when I
visited Surnadal, a community about 75 miles southwest of Trondheim.
King Christian V (1670-1699) travelled from Copenhagen to that
Norwegian valley in the summer of 1685. The king presented a plaque
to the people which now hangs in the Mo Church. As an American
whose family left there in 1892, I was surprised at the importance still
attached to that "ancient" event. The point was that both Denmark and
Norway seemed to believe that they would stay together forever.

The political destiny of my ancestral valley, however, was to change
radically by new events taking place on the continent of Europe.
Napoleon was on the march to conquer the world. Except for a bad
winter in Russia, he might have succeeded. Napoleon ordered his marshall, Jean Baptiste Jules Bernadotte, to occupy Denmark if the Danes
would not declare war on England. King Frederick VI (1808-1839) was
immediately confronted with an English counter-threat. After weighing
his unhappy choices, the Danish king cast his lot with Napoleon. He
concluded that Denmark had more to fear from the French armies than
from the English navy. On April 12, 1801, Lord Nelson directed the
British bombardment of Copenhagen. The Danish navy was destroyed
and its merchant ships were taken to England as prizes of war. The
Danes were never compensated. It also meant that Norway was cut off
from Denmark and suffered severely from a blockade.

Another surprise took place. Sweden's royal house of Vasa had run

19

out of heirs. In searching about for new royalty, they elected Marshall Bernadotte as crown prince, to the pleasure of Napoleon. The French emperor privately disliked and feared the marshall and this was an opportunity to send him to Sweden. It could also provide him with an ally against England and Russia. Once in Sweden, Bernadotte switched sides. He joined the enemies of Napoleon. His reward was Norway. At the Treaty of Kiel, signed on Jan. 14, 1814, Denmark gave up Norway to Sweden under threat from the "super-powers." It was to be Sweden's compensation for its loss of Finland to Russia just a few years before. The French marshall was secretly wishing for Napoleon's defeat and hoped that he would become the new king of France. He had accepted the Swedish offer with some private reservations. When that time came, however, the French chose their new king from the House of Bourbon.

Bernadotte chose the name of Karl XIV Johan. English historians call him Charles John. The main street in Oslo leading from the palace to the parliament building is called "Karl Johansgate." He never did learn to speak Swedish, much less Norwegian. His son, Oscar I, and his grandson, Oscar II also served as kings of both Sweden and Norway. The Bernadottes are the royal family of Sweden today and Karl XVI Gustaf is dearly loved as a true Swede.

History ought to be read like a detective novel or a mystery story. One of the mysteries to me has been why so many Norwegian families named their sons "Oscar." Afterall, Norway had been forced into accepting a Swedish ruler by military threat. Besides, I'd heard some things as a young boy that Swedes and Norwegians were supposed to be "cool" towards each other. Why then did so many Norse immigrant familes name their sons after King Oscar who lived in Stockholm?

I think I have found the answer. Oscar II was king of Norway from 1872 to 1905, when he resigned the Norwegian throne. He lived two more years as the king of Sweden. That was the main emigrant period from Norway to America. He was a popular king in Norway and had been called the "Norwegian prince." Immigrant families honored King Oscar naming their sons after him.

There may be another reason too. In my home community, almost every family had a son named "Oscar." I learned that a great many of these immigrants were from Trondelag, the area around Trondheim (it was called "Trondhjem" until 1930). D. K. Derry, an English historian who lives in Oslo, has pointed out that the early migration into Trondelag had come by way of Sweden and there has always been a pro-Swedish sentiment in that part of Norway.

So one of the great mysteries of my childhood is now solved. I now know why my father was named "Oscar." If he ever knew the reason, he never told me. And I suspect that he lived his whole life quite unaware of the "French connection."

Ole Alvsen Fiske (1840-1890).

CHAPTER 8

"Syttende Mai"—
Norway's Constitution Day

MAY 17 - "SYTTENDE MAI" - is Norway's happiest holiday. How did it start and what does it mean? On that day in 1814, 112 men signed a new constitution for Norway. They had been elected from the Lutheran state church parishes. They had travelled by foot, skis, horseback and wagons from every part of Norway except the far northern parts, Nordland and Finnmark. Travel was not possible from those wintry areas. The delegates met at Eidsvoll in the home of Carsten Anker, a wealthy merchant. Eidsvoll is about 40 miles north of Oslo.

The constitutional assembly met for worship on Easter Sunday. It consisted of 47 officials, 37 farmers, 16 town representatives and 12 from the military. It was called by Christian Frederick, the ruling representative of the Danish king. The purpose of the assembly was to save Norway from an uncertain future. The majority of the delegates favored declaring Norway an independent monarchy with the Prince Christian Frederick as the new monarch. He was not unwilling.

It was an age of revolutions and a time for redrawing the maps of Europe and the New World. A new nation, the United States of America, had adopted a constitution in 1787 based on freedom and justice for all. The might of Britain had been repulsed. In France too, a once powerful monarchy had been overthrown and a new constitution was adopted in 1791.

An international crisis had started the chain of events rolling. As "punishment" for siding with the French, England and its allies had forced the Danish king to give up claim to Norway at the Treaty of Kiel on Jan. 14, 1814. This ended a joint rule begun in 1380 and which lasted 434 years. The Norwegians had not even been consulted! Ironically, Norway's possessions, Iceland, Greenland the Faroe Islands, were overlooked in the treaty and became Danish colonies by default. Norway was promised to Sweden as compensation for the loss of Finland to Russia in 1809.

The Eidsvoll assembly was a bold stroke for independence. Why couldn't Norway be free? The delegates studied the new American and French constitutions. It was also known that Karl Johan of the Bernadotte family in France, who had become Sweden's new crown prince in 1810, would rather have returned to France as its new king rather than wait for his future in Sweden. He never did learn the Swedish language. The French, however, restored the Bourbon family to power and Karl Johan chose to cash in on his fortune in Sweden with Norway as a bonus.

Brave talk, however, is not enough to secure freedom. The British navy blockaded Norway and cut off its needed food supplies as well as all exports. The economy crumbled. By the end of July, Karl Johan personally took command of his battle hardened troops. They were superior to Norway's "home guard" in numbers, training and equipment. Fighting lasted less than two weeks. The pro-Swedish faction in Norway's Storting (parliament), headed by Herman Wedel Jarlsberg, held sway. They were no less patriotic, but were realists about international politics. During this time, they were also lobbying in London for more favorable terms. Christian Frederick renounced his claim to be king of Norway and returned to his homeland where he became King Christian VIII, 25 years later. On Nov. 4, 1814, the Storting unanimously elected and recognized Karl XIII, the king of Sweden, as Norway's monarch. Norway, however, remained a separate nation from Sweden and was only beholden to the king.

The Norwegians negotiated a favorable agreement with their new king. The constitution was respected, they were not required to supply troops for Sweden's foreign wars, they could elect and run their own Storting and a representative of the king would reside in Oslo.

Four years later, the French-born Crown Prince of Sweden became King Karl XIV Johan. He would liked to have had Nov. 4 celebrated as a holiday in Norway in recognition of his rule. As in so many things proposed by the Swedish kings, the Norwegians were not agreeable. Instead, a group of students led a demonstration on May 17, 1829, a symbol of their determination for full Norwegian freedom. Still hoping to win the Norsemen over, the king good naturedly allowed "Syttende Mai" to be celebrated.

The "Unions Perioden," as the union with Sweden was called, lasted until Oct. 26, 1905, when the Swedish King Oscar II gave up all rights to Norway. He concluded that it was a hopeless task to govern Norway from Sweden. It was also a time of bad economy and heavy emigration to the New World.

"Syttende Mai" has become as much a symbol of freedom to Norwegians as July 4 to Americans. Norsemen are still celebrating May 17 as their Constitution Day, even though independence didn't come for another 91 years. When independence finally came in 1905, they revised and updated the Eidsvoll constitution and declared it to be "Kongeriget Norges Nye Grundlov" (the Kingdom of Norway's New Constitution). The Eidsvoll assembly had done its work well. Long live the constitution and freedom for Norsemen and their neighbors everywhere!

CHAPTER 9

"Call Her Nettie Olson"—
An Immigrant Family's Story

T HE "LITTLE HOUSE ON THE PRAIRIE" was often too small for the immigrant family. This proved to be a challenge to Andrene's family which had emigrated from Hemsedal, a part of Hallingdal in Norway. Like so many others from that valley in the county of Buskerud, they settled first at Blooming Prairie in southeast Minnesota. It is said that all 1400 people living in the city spoke "Halling," besides the many farm families for miles around.

The war between the states was over. Norway, together with other western European lands, had "America Fever." The government was alarmed that so many of its labor force wanted to leave. The State Church issued warnings to the people about the dangers which they faced if they went to that uncivilized and heathen land. If they escaped being mugged in New York, they would surely be met by "Savages" waiting for their scalps on the prairies and in the woodlands. They were forcefully advised that they would be leaving behind both family and God, if they went to America.

Threats did not keep people from seeking passage to the New World. They bought the cheapest fares. For about $50 or $60, a person could travel from Norway to Iowa and Minnesota. There were tears as the last glimpse of the "old country" faded from their eyes. Later they would sing, "Kan du glemme gamle Norge?" ("Can you forget old Norway?") After a brief stop at Newcastle and Liverpool, England, they saw no land until they docked in New York City's harbor.

There were no fond memories of their quarters in the steerage section of the boats. The food was equally bad and it did no good to complain. To the shipowners, immigrants were simply "cargo," not much different than if they had been cattle. Nor were they safe from attacks by the ship's crew. Women stayed in the protection of their men. The smell and disease were sickening, not to mention rats. It was not uncommon to die at sea in such conditions.

THE SCANDINAVIAN HERITAGE

Ole and Kari Bakken were among those who came to Blooming Prairie in 1867. Their name had been "Hølle" in Norway. They settled on a farm near the Red Oak Grove Lutheran Church. Andrene was the youngest of their six children. One Sunday, they were visiting the nearby farm of Uncle Knute and Aunt Guri. When it was time to go home, Andrene, just six years old, was nowhere to be found. After an anxious search, she was discovered asleep in the tall grass by the railroad tracks.

Now Knute and Guri had no children. Their only child had died. This was not an unusual thing in those days. Guri was the one who found the missing Andrene. When she returned with her to the farm, she announced: "Because I found her, she is going to be my little girl. Besides, you already have enough children!" Nothing would change her mind, Andrene would replace the child that had died. Finally, Ole and Kari yielded. They thought it might be good for Guri to have a little girl in her home. Besides, the Bakken house was getting crowded. Andrene, however, wasn't happy with the arrangement. It didn't take her long to decide that what Aunt Guri really wanted was someone to do the chores. She'd run home to her parents so she could play with her sisters. Then Guri would come with a stick and order her to return.

The Bakkens had three sons and needed more land. This was not easy to find in the Blooming Prairie community. In 1879, they moved to a site west of Walcott in southeastern North Dakota where many other Hallings were settling. Their oldest daughter, Anna, remained behind to be married. Andrene chose to stay with her. This was a happy period in her life. When it came time to enroll in school, a neighbor girl took her along. She was asked by the teacher, "What is your friend's name?" After a pause, she answered, "Call her Nettie Olson." And Nettie Olson it was for many years. She was a good listener and had a deep love for learning. She had a special ability for memory work and qualified herself to be a teacher.

There wasn't much "romance" to life on the prairie in those days. It was mostly harsh survival. Houses were built without insulation and stood as stark silhouettes against the horizons. It took years before the groves of trees grew up to give protection against the elements. Conditions were far different from Norway. The summer heat was intense. Bugs, flies and other insects were everywhere. Milk soured quickly and it was impossible to make cheese or butter when gnats filled the air. Lightning storms were particularly loud and frightening. Rattlesnakes were often found in the fields. The greatest terror came from prairie fires. In the dry weather and with a hard wind, it took no time for a field to become a sea of flames. The fires moved so quickly that the fastest horse could not outrun their fury. Travelers carried matches to light backfires as a way of protecting themselves. The winter blizzards also tested the endurance of the strongest settlers and there was very little money.

The Red Oak Church became a source of inspiration for Andrene. She memorized long sections of the Bible and loved to sing hymns, ballads and folk songs which she had learned by heart. One of the famous pioneer pastors was in the Blooming Prairie community from 1875-83. He was Rev. Claus Clausen. A native of Denmark, he ministered among Norwegians. Earlier he had been at Muskego, near Milwaukee, one of the earliest Norwegian settlements in the New World.

Andrene married Hellik Thoreson (renamed Thompson) from Lyngdal in Numedal, west of Oslo. After living a few years by Doran, Minnesota, they moved near her family by Walcott where they reared seven children. When she was married, she reclaimed her name, "Andrene," but I will always affectionately remember her as "Grandma."

CHAPTER 10

Snorri Sturluson:
Iceland's "Royal Storyteller"

THOSE OF US WHO LOVE the Scandinavian heritage owe a great debt to Snorri Sturluson, Iceland's most famous saga writer. A saga is a story, usually based on facts, which tends to grow a little as it is re-told. Who was Snorri and how did he become so famous?

Iceland is an unusual place. According to geologists, it is the newest country in the world. It was formed through a series of volcanic eruptions "only" 20 million years ago. Kathleen Schermann, who wrote a delightful book on Iceland, called it "Daughter of Fire." Its earliest name was "Thule," given by a French navigator in 330 B.C. Roman coins minted between 270-305 A.D. have been found on the island, indicating that the Roman navy stationed in Britain had visited there.

The first known inhabitants of Iceland were Irish monks in search of solitude during the seventh century. It was, however, the Norwegians coming in large numbers during the late ninth century who built the colonies which still exist. Despite its closeness to the Arctic Circle, Iceland was a hospitable site for settlers. Its temperature was two degrees warmer then and 24 percent of its surface was covered by trees. There are very few trees in Iceland today.

The original Norwegian settlers were of very proud and capable stock. They left their native land because of the oppression of civil rights by King Harald Haarfagre. This caused the landowners to pack their belongings in their "knorrs," a Viking cargo ship. In Iceland they laid the foundations for the world's oldest democracy.

The Sturlusons were latecomers among the chieftain families of the island. Snorri was born in 1178 to a minor chieftain named Sturla. His grandmother, however, had descended from Egil Skallagrimsson, the greatest scaldic poet of the land.

Though a gentle man himself, Snorri's life was turbulent. He was constantly involved in feuds, lawsuits and politics. When Snorri was three, a famous judge, Jon Luftsson, became his "foster father." This was not unusual in those days. Jon's grandfather, Saemund the Learned, had studied in France and had founded a famous cultural center at Oddi in southern Iceland. He had written a history of the Norse kings in Latin. Jon's mother was an illegitimate daughter of King Magnus Bareleg of Norway. (The matter of irregular birth was not a social handicap among Vikings.) This placed Snorri into a position for social climbing.

When Snorri was only five, his father died and left him little inheritance. His foster father died when he was 19, leaving him an education. He gained his wealth and power by good business skills, family support and favorable marriages. At 21, Snorri married the daughter of a wealthy farmer. Three years later, the farmer died and Snorri became a rich chieftain. Then he contracted to take care of an elderly farmer with a large estate which became his. Among his wives and mistresses was the wealthiest widow in Iceland. He also married off his daughters to politically influential families.

In politics, Snorri advanced quickly. At 35, he was elected "Lawspeaker," the highest office in the land. This required a thorough knowledge of legal matters. His education at Oddi was not wasted. Having succeeded so well in Iceland, Snorri next tried to establish his fame with the kings of Norway. In the style of the times, he wrote poetry to flatter the people from whom he wished favors. All went well for a while. It brought him gifts and titles. But absolutist kings give nothing for free. Each time Snorri received recognition, his political position in Iceland was compromised. The Icelanders had good memories. They knew that their freedom was safest when the Norse rulers were looking in other directions.

Finally, the very sucess which he had purchased through marriages and favors turned against him. Two of his sons-in-law, having feuded with Snorri about land, became agents of Norway's King Haakon. They were ordered by the king to either arrest Snorri and return him to Norway, or kill him if he resisted. They chose to murder him on his farm. He was 61 years old.

So why do we remember Snorri Sturluson? He has written the sagas of the Norse kings called "Heimskringla." It is our best source of

29

information on the Viking age. His style is gripping, even in translation. Basic to his writing was the belief in the sainthood of King Olaf Haraldsson which has remained a central feature of Norwegian Christianity.

It is ironic that the Icelanders, themselves refugees from Norway, became the recorders of a major part of the Scandinavian heritage. What's more, the Icelanders are the only people in the world today who still speak a language similar to the "Old Norse" of the Viking days.

Arbaejar Folk Museum, Reykjavik, Iceland.

CHAPTER 11

The Norse Gods—
Where Have They Gone?

WITH A MIGHTY SWING OF A CLUB, King Olaf Haralds-son is said to have smashed the image of Thor and crushed the pagan power over Norway. Who was Thor and who were the other gods of the Norse pantheon? What was there about them which was so repulsive to Christians? Did Olaf really return them to Valhalla forever?

In the Viking world of 1000 years ago, the presence of the ancient Germanic gods in their Scandinavian forms had a powerful influence. The main deities were Odin, Thor and Frey. Each was held to have his sphere of power. Odin was the chief god called the "All-Father." His was the dark world of death. Human sacrifice of enemies, individuals and whole armies was common. Even his devotees were claimed on feast days. His home was in a mythological "Asgard," also the location of Valhalla, reserved for the bravest men who died gloriously in battle. He was also the god of poetry and wisdom. In zeal for knowledge, he sacrificed one of his eyes. He is credited with having discovered the 16 letters of the runic writings called "futhark." Two ravens attended him and brought him the news of the world.

Thor was the most popular god. He is best known for his hammer and the thunder it produced. Thor was the god of the seamen and farmers. He was a giant with red hair, beard and eyes, and traversed the heavens in a chariot pulled by two sacred goats. Wherever he rode, lightning flashed and thunder roared. His hammer became a goodluck charm given as a wedding present to insure fertility.

The third god in the Norse trinity was Frey. In the sagas, we read that "Frey is the noblest of the gods. He controls the rain and sunshine and therefore the natural increase of the earth, and it is good to call upon him for fruitful season and for peace. He also controls the good fortunes of men." With his twin sister, Freyja, they had a lewd and lustful in-fluence on the morals of their times. Frey was the chief god of the Swedes and was the divine ancestor of the royal family at Uppsala.

THE SCANDINAVIAN HERITAGE

From where did these gods come? Snorri Sturluson, Iceland's great saga writer, offered an explanation. In the opening lines of his story of the Norse kings called "Heimskringla," he claimed that the "gods" had been Asiatic kings. They were pictured as physically large and mighty in power. They were supposed to have great wisdom and were skilled in magic. He held that after the Flood, most of Noah's descendants forgot their earlier knowledge of the true God. Instead, they deified the earth and the heavenly bodies. In their amazement at the wonders of the earth, they related these powers to the kings of the east. Priam of Troy and other notables were thought to be their ancestors.

Snorri did not invent the stories. As an intellectual Christian scholar and chieftain, he popularized the legends preserved in older stories. A basic source was called the "Elder Edda" which was rooted in the pre-Viking world of Germanic legend. It included heroes such as Sigurd the Dragon-Slayer, Attila the Hun and Ermaneric the Goth. Names such as Brynhild, Gudron and Gunnar have survived from these legends. The Valkyries of Wagnerian opera were the warrior companions of Odin.

The dream of Vahalla was the inspiration of the Viking warriors as they plunged into battle. It was especially the "berserks" who threw aside all caution to claim carnage for their gods. They expected the Valkyries to serve them endless amounts of ale every evening as they returned from battle, while their wounds were miraculously healed.

The struggle between Christians and pagans in Scandinavia was not always total virtue vs. total depravity, but the seeds for peace did take root after many generations. Note the fact that Trygve Lie of Norway and Dag Hamarskjold of Sweden were the first two Secretary Generals of the United Nations.

Are the Norse gods all gone? Imagine my surprise when I learned a few years ago that my maternal grandfather was born "Thoresen" ("son of Thor") and not "Thompson," as I had supposed. On entering the New World, he exorcized his name of its ancient past to begin life in America as "son of Thomas," the Apostle.

But don't think that we are through with these gods. Every week they pass through the heavens as Wednesday (Odin's day), Thursday (Thor's day) and Friday (Frey's day). Besides these better known gods, Tuesday is named after Tyr (Anglo-Saxon "Tiu"), a war god. Though officially discredited, they die hard and still influence the value systems of society.

CHAPTER 12

Leif Erikson
Discovers America!

WHO REALLY DISCOVERED AMERICA? As a child, I was taught in school that it was found in 1492 by an Italian named Christopher Columbus. There was also a rumor in my home community that a Norwegian had found it long before that Columbus fellow, whoever he was. Recently, Great Britain's Royal Geographical Society reports that a Welshman, John Lloyd, who was trading with the Vikings in Greenland, reached America in 1475 while searching for the fabled "Northwest Passage" to China. Because the trading was illegal, the information was kept secret at the time and later passed on to John Cabot.

This can become quite an emotional issue. Andy Anderson, the founder and president of the "Leif Erikson Society" in Chicago, has been on a truth campaign to set the record straight. He published a book entitled "Viking Explorers and the Columbus Fraud." There is no question in his mind where credit ought to go for finding this New World. In fact, he musters up quite a few arguments to assert that the whole Columbus story is a case of mistaken identity. He claims that the real "Columbus" was a Jewish seafarer from Spain named Christobal Colon. As you can guess, Anderson is not the darling of Italian-Americans.

What is the case for claiming that Leif got here first? There are three main sources. First, Snorri Sturluson, the famous Icelandic saga writer, wrote of Leif: "He...found Vinland the Good." Second, a story called the "Tale of the Greenlanders." And third, the "Saga of Erik the Red." These writings do not always agree on all points. Erik (Old Norse did not have the letter "c"), also spelled "Eirik," was the father of Leif who was called the "Lucky." Erik had been outlawed in Iceland because of his pagan ways with the sword in settling personal disputes. Fleeing Iceland, he established a colony on the west coast of Greenland which grew into at least 330 known farm sites. Norsemen continued to live in Greenland for over 400 years. That's longer than they've been in North Dakota!

America may have been first seen by Europeans when a Viking boat was blown off course en route to Greenland from Iceland. The Viking ships did not do too well against hard winds with their single sails, though they rode the waves well. The leader, Bjarni Herjolfsson, did not stop to explore the land but turned back to Greenland to tell his story to Erik. Leif bought Bjarni's ship and with a crew of 35 set sail westward about the year 1003. Their first landing was among glaciers, probably Baffin Island, which he named "Helluland."

The second landing was named "Markland" or "Land of Forests" and was likely Labrador. The place which lived on in their memories, however, was named Vinland because so many grapes were found. On board ship was a German winemaker. He became ecstatic at the sight. Wine was expensive in Greenland because it had to be imported from Europe. Here was a paradise of unlimited grapes and abundant salmon in the lakes and streams.

Leif returned to Greenland and became its ruler. He is also credited with converting the people to be Christians. Leif himself became a Christian while visiting King Olaf Tryggvason in Norway. Olaf was an uncompromising evangelist.

The task of colonizing the New World was taken up by Leif's brother Thorvald. All went well at first. But on his first contact with "Native Americans," there was bloodshed. The Norsemen acted arrogantly. One of the natives escaped and returned with an attacking force. An avenging arrow killed Thorvald and the rest fled in their boats. He was the first European to be buried in America.

Besides the saga accounts, is there any other evidence that Norsemen set foot on American soil 500 years before Columbus? Attempts have been made to locate Norse settlements all the way from Hudson Bay to Virginia. But there is only one place which many scholars agree is clearly identified. It's on the northern tip of Newfoundland called "L'Anse aux Meadows." Helge Ingstad, a Norwegian Arctic explorer, began excavating in 1961. His findings were confirmed by Dr. Bengt Schonback, an eminent Swedish archaeologist. Evidence of buildings, jewelry, tools, slag iron and coal have been found.

A much publicized map purchased by Yale University has turned out to be highly controversial. Many claim it's a fraud. In 1898, a stone slab written in runic letters was found near Kensington, MN. It told of 30

Scandinavians who had journeyed inland and met tragedy. Most scholars, however, reject the genuiness of the stone. But this has not discouraged nearby Alexandria from erecting a monument to display for tourists. Perhaps other runic slabs will be found and Leif's claim for finding America will turn up some new wrinkles.

CHAPTER 13

Ole, The Cotter's Son—
A Story Of Courage And Love

THERE ARE MANY COTTER'S SONS who left the Old World for the New. Their departure did not mean a lack of love for parents or native land. They left because they had a desperate dream for a better life.

A "cotter" (husmann) was a share-cropper who had a cottage on the edge of the main farm. It was often on a hillside and had to first be reclaimed by removing rocks. But this was the only way that a young man could have a home. He could not, of course, expect to accumulate savings. Most of his time was spent working for the landowner, called a "bønde." I have seen these hillside huts. They may look pretty, but they are humble shelters.

Hans Anderson Foss wrote a story called "Husmandsgutten" or "The Cotter's Son." It was first serialized by the Decorah-Posten in 1884 and was claimed to be the most read book written by a Norwegian-American.

The story is about Ole Haugen, born in the Sigdal area west of Oslo. (A "haug" is a hill or hillside. This accounts for his last name.) His parents, Torkil and Randi, were cotters on the land of the wealthiest farmer in the valley. The bønde was a hard man, but his wife was known for her kindness.

The custom in those days was that when there was a baptism or confirmation that the request to the pastor had to be accompanied by a gift of money. It was not unlike the Levitical laws of the Old Testament which prescribed sacrifices. Like Joseph and Mary who could give only a poor family's offering when their son was brought to the Temple, Ole's parents also struggled to provide the prescribed gift. The bønde refused to give Torkil a loan for the baptism, so his wife secretly sent some of her own silver coins to them. The bønde's rule was: "The more you give them, the more they want and the less they will work."

Ole amazed everyone at his confirmation with his sincere and quick answers during the catechization. This was a custom where children publicly recited their knowledge of the Bible and their faith. Some people thought that Ole should be a minister and raised money to send him to school. The bønde, however, put a stop to that. To complicate matters more, the bønde's daughter, Marie, was the same age as Ole. They played together as children and became fast friends. To separate them, Ole was sent up to the seter (mountain pasture) early in the spring. There he stayed wth the farm animals until just before snowfall when he returned for school. The bønde was taking no chances. He didn't want his money to fall into a cotter's family.

Despite the attempts to keep them apart, Ole and Marie came to have a deep love for each other. They realized that the only hope they had for a future together was if Ole went to America. So he went. His best friend in the New World was Nils, also from Norway. He had a brilliant head for business, but was a constant failure to say "no" to the bottle. Ole's friendship gave him the new directions that he needed. He later repaid with good business advice.

It was Ole's intention to send money back to his family and then return to Marie. In his first job, west of Chicago, he was cheated out of wages for the whole summer. So he set out on foot to look for work in Wisconsin, as winter approached. On the way, he was mistaken for a bank robber and was arrested. After his innocence was proved, he was released and nearly lost his life in a snow storm north of Madison. He found refuge wih an American family who also gave him a job on their farm. During a sudden winter storm, Ole rescued the family's two teenage daughters at great risk to himself. He carried them to their home in a blinding blizzard. The farm dog led him. One of the daughters, Nellie, survived.

The neighbors, of course, began to talk. Ole's brave deed got into the newspapers and was reprinted in Norway. It also said that Ole was going to marry Nellie! This was all the bønde needed to see. He showed it to Marie, but she refused to believe it. Then the bønde intercepted the mail so that there was no correspondence between Ole and his family or with Marie for a year and a half. Money sent home was also stolen by the bønde.

Stories like this were not uncommon, but not all of them had happy endings. In this case, the love between Ole and Marie stood the test. With the help of Nils, Ole made a good business investment in Chicago that made it possible to go back to Norway with lots of money in his pocket. The high point in the story is when Ole bought the bønde's farm at an auction. The mail fraud had caught up with the rich farmer and he died a poor man.

The story has more pathos than can be retold here. But stories like this from the Sigdal-Numedal area have been preserved as a reminder to the children of immigrants that courage and love still have their rewards.

CHAPTER 14

Vikings Attack Lindisfarne, Britain's "Holy Island"

"FROM THE FURY OF THE NORTHMEN, O Lord, deliver us." These words are alleged to have been prayed in the churches of France during the "Viking Age" (793-1066). While no copy of such a prayer exists, it certainly was the sentiment lifted up from the Christian altars in those fearful times.

The Viking "breakout" was a long time in preparation. Over-population, the inheritance rights of the oldest sons and the excitement of adventure combined with new technologies to produce such times. It came on June 8, 793. The target was Lindisfarne, a bare and windswept island to the northeast of York in England. Lindisfarne was the home of peaceful monks who went about their duties of chores, prayers and scholarship. The monastery was famous for its "illuminated gospels," considered to be the most beautiful book ever produced.

All of a sudden, the Viking longships appeared with their square sails and dragon heads. A contemporary historian wrote: "And they came to the church of Lindisfarne, laid everything waste with grievous plunderings, trampled the holy places with with polluted feet, dug up the altars and seized all the treasures of the holy church. They killed some of the brothers; some they took away with them in fetters; many they drove out, naked and loaded with insults; and some they drowned in the sea." After Lindisfarne, every monastery and abbey in England, Scotland and Ireland was fair game for a raid. In another six years, France would also feel this new fury.

Lindisfarne was thought to be so holy that no harm could come to it. Missionaries from another holy island, Iona, on the west coast of Scotland, had founded this center of piety and learning. From the invader's point of view, it was easy picking. Monasteries were banks for the local wealth and had no guards or military fortifications. The attack on Lindisfarne sent shock waves across Europe. Besides, no one believed that the sea could be crossed over such a long distance:

After the attack, churchmen of the time claimed that there had been heavenly warnings: "...exceptional flashes of lightning, and fiery dragons were seen flying in the air," followed by famine. Alcuin, a famous English scholar teaching in the courts of Emperor Charlemagne in France, claimed that the attack came as a punishment for the sins of England! In addition to adultery, dishonesty and injustice, he also cited "long hair and flashy clothing."

But what made the raid possible? It was the Viking longship. It is fortunate for us that several of these ships have been preserved in the cold blue clay of Norway. These were buried in the earth as "coffins" for wealthy chieftains—often accompanied by slaves, animals and favorite spouse! One of these is called the "Gokstad" ship, found southwest of Oslo. It is now on display at the Viking Ship Museum at Bygdøy Park in Oslo. Every traveller to Oslo should visit this museum.

The Gokstad ship was used for both peace and war. It could travel up shallow rivers and could be either sailed or rowed. Thirty-two oarsmen worked at a time. Double crews would ensure "non-stop" travel.

The "Hjemkomst" which sailed to Norway from Duluth, Minnesota, in 1983, was modelled after the Gokstad ship. Built in a potato warehouse in Hawley, Minnesota, by the late Robert Asp, it is 76½ feet long. It captured the attention of the world during its famous "homecoming" voyage. Magnus Magnusson, the archaeologist and writer who created and narrated the PBS-TV series "Vikings!," said: "To my mind, quite simply, Gokstad is the most beautiful ship ever built." The Hjemkomst is now in a museum in Moorhead, Minnesota.

The attack on Lindisfarne raised some serious questions. First, did the Viking attacks prove that Odin and Thor were more powerful than the "White Christ?" Taken at face value, it would seem so. Yet in another 200 years, Norway itself would come under the sway of missionaries from England.

A second question: Is military preparation a contradiction to faith in God? Is it true, as a peace conference speaker said: "If God is on our side, why do we need the biggest weapons?"

The Gokstad ship is now a harmless museum piece, but it is also a grim reminder of the role which advanced technology plays in both peace and war. Lindisfarne, Britain's "holy island," might well be remembered as we struggle with the same hard realities in our time.

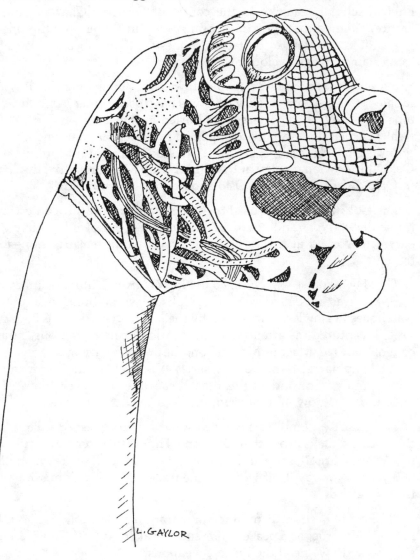

From the Oseberg ship, Bygdøy (Oslo).

CHAPTER 15

The Vikings
In Russia

IT WAS MAINLY THE SWEDISH VIKINGS that travelled the rivers of Russia. In fact, "Russia" was once known as "Greater Sweden." The "Rus" of the Viking Age were Scandinavians. They were also known as "Varangians."

A great deal of mystery enshrouds the sagas of the Vikings in Russia. The traditional view has been based on the "Russian Primary Chronicle," written during the 12th century in a monastery near Kiev. Although Swedish travel and trade began at least by 650, it was about 860 when the "Rus" were invited to Russia by the leaders of Kiev. The "Chronicle" states: "Let us find a king to rule over us and make judgments according to the law, for our land is large and rich, but there is no order in it. So come and be king over us."

One of those who came was Rurik. He is identified with the founding of Novgorod. The Hermitage Museum in Leningrad, once the Winter Palace of the Czars, has a large collection of Viking artifacts. There is no doubt that Vikings were in Russia. But what did they do and how important were their contributions?

In addition to Russian and Scandinavian records, there were also contemporary Arab accounts. Ibn Fadlan wrote: "I have seen the Rus as they come on their merchant journeys, and stay encamped on the Volga. I have never seen more perfect specimens, tall as date palms, blonde and ruddy. Each man has an axe, a sword and a knife which he keeps by him at all times. Each woman wears neck rings of gold and silver, one for each thousand dinars her master owns." An Arab geographer, Ibn Rustah, described the Rus as traders in furs and slaves. He noted that they wore clean clothing and were hospitable to strangers. He was shocked, however, at their funeral practice of burying alive the favorite wife of a chief with him in his grave.

Unlike the Danes and Norwegians who settled as farmers in England, Ireland and France, the Swedes in Russia were interested primarily in trade. One of the great Rus leaders in Kiev was Oleg. In 907, he attacked Constantinople and forced the Greek Emperor to make a treaty giving the Rus trade advantages, including entry visas, customs duties and access to markets and supplies. He also got the Greeks to agree that the Rus should be given as many free baths as they wanted. Despite their bad press, the Scandianvians were a clean living race.

The best known of the Rus leaders was Vladimir (Valdemar), the first Christian ruler of Russia and the great grandson of Rurik. With help from Scandinavian allies, he conquered his rivals and consolidated a Russian kingdom stretching from Poland to the Volga.

In 988, while Sweden was still pagan, Vladimir converted to Christianity when he married Anna, sister to the Greek emperor. It is significant that he made the Slavic language official for church use, rather than Greek or Norse. This made Christianity a "native" rather than a "foreign" religion.

There was a close relationship between Scandinavia and Russia in those days. Both King Olaf Tryggvason and Olaf Haraldsson (St. Olaf) spent times as exiles in Russia. Vladimir is honored not only in the Russian Orthodox Church, but is also listed on July 15, the day of his death, on the calendar of festivals in the "Lutheran Book of Worship."

His conversion to Christianity was uncompromising. He put away his 800 mistresses, destroyed his idols and became a great builder of churches. Kiev alone had 350 churches. It is perhaps not strange that he died in a battle in which his former wives and their sons rose up against him in 1015.

As time went on, the Vikings in Russia accepted the native Slavic customs. They have done the same in England, France, Ireland, Italy and also in America. The last famous Scandinavian ruler of Russia was Yaroslav who built its first cathedral, St. Sophia, modelled after the famous church in Constantinople.

You should know, however, that modern Soviet historians have a different interpretation of the importance of the Norse presence. A famous Moscow archaeologist stated: "The role of the Vikings in the formation of the Russian State was rather small." It may be that the western view is glossed with some romantic mythology. There are those, however, who interpret this "downplay" as typical Soviet revisionism and Slavic chauvinism.. But in any case, the Viking saga in Russia is made more fascinating by the mystery which surrounds it.

CHAPTER 16

"Fourth Of July"
Celebrated In Denmark

THE LARGEST CELEBRATION of American Independence outside the USA is observed in the wooded and heather-clad hills of Rebild, in Denmark. Crowds up to 40,000 people gather in a park about 15 miles south of Aalborg in northern Jutland.

It began in 1912 and has continued every year except for the two world wars when Denmark was isolated. The land was purchased by a group of Americans of Danish descent and is now under the auspices of the Rebild National Park Society.

Scandinavians have been intensely patriotic Americans, but they have not lost their love for the lands of their origins. This colorful celebration in Denmark is no exception. At the first festival in 1912, 10,000 people attended, headed by King Christian X and Queen Alexandrine, despite a pouring rain.

One of the most colorful founders of the event was Dr. Max Henius. He was the son of Jewish parents who had come to Denmark from Poland. After completing a doctorate at Marburg University in Germany, he moved to Chicago. As a scientist, he took a keen interest in public health. When a typhus epidemic broke out in that city in 1892, he traced the problem to sewage disposal in Lake Michigan. He also learned that water taken from the lake and given to a tubercular cow had helped spread the epidemic.

Dr. Henius came to love America and worked to bring together people from both sides of the Atlantic who knit the ties between the two countries. He died in 1935 after receiving many honors. He is remembered in Denmark today as the "Great Originator."

The Fourth of July in Denmark is a highly festival day. Rebild itself is an especially beautiful park. It is one of those rare places in the nation where there are tree covered hills. The luscious green of the trees and grass offers a lovely setting for a picnic at any time of the summer, but on no day is there such excitement as on July 4. People begin arriving early in the morning to find their favorite spot for a blanket, cushions and lawn chairs. The United States Air Force Band of Europe is flown in from England to perform. Special speakers, representing both Denmark and the USA are on hand. Among such notables have been Earl Warren, Walt Disney, Ralph Bunch, Hubert Humphrey, Danny Kaye, Edsel Ford Jr., and Richard Nixon (before he became president).

The Rebild National Park Society which sponsors the celebration is a non-political organization with chapters in Denmark and the United States. There is even a chapter in Greenland with about 100 members, including some United States Army personnel. There are about 10 active chapters, according to Mr. Ejnar Danielson, president of the Chicago Rebild Chapter. Having as their goal to perpetuate the strong ties of friendship between the two countries, they especially try to instill a feeling of love for Denmark among younger Danish-Americans.

According to "Den Danske Pioneer," a Danish-American newspaper published in Chicago (July 12, 1982), 1,700,000 Americans claim Danish roots. Over 26 percent of Danish-Americans list Denmark as their ethnic homeland. There are, of course, many more who are part Danish but have claimed some other ethnic identification. Altogether, "Den Danske Pioneer" reports that over 11 million Americans claim Scandinavian derivation. It is only since the large immigrations after the Civil War in the USA, however, that Scandinavians have made a point to identify with their ethnic heritage. The 1980 US census gave the following total of Scandinavians who reported at least one specific ancestry group: Danish—1,518,273; Finnish 615,872; Icelandic—32,586; Norwegian—3,453,839; and Swedish—4,345,392. Another 475,007 reported "Scandinavian." Some estimates place the total Scandinavian population in North America at around 20,000,000.

Abraham Lincoln has long been a hero to the Scandinavians. At Rebild, there is a log cabin museum built in his honor with logs from every state in the USA in which Danes live. Dedicated in 1934, it houses the mementos of Danish immigrants to America. Included are old photos of Danes and their American homes, early household utensils, documents and even a covered wagon like those used in the westward trek through the Great Plains.

THE SCANDINAVIAN HERITAGE

If you are ever in Denmark on the Fourth of July, plan to visit Rebild. But come early and bring a picnic lunch and an umbrella, just in case it rains. It was a beautiful day when our family were there to celebrate. It made us proud to be both Scandinavians and Americans.

Danish windmill.

CHAPTER 17

Norwegian Folk
Tales—Retold

"IF NORWAY WERE TO SHOW THE WORLD a single work of art which would most truly express the Norwegian character, perhaps the best choice would be the folk tales," wrote Pat Shaw Iverson, a recognized writer of Norwegian stories.

Two names are especially remembered in the collecting of these tales. Peter Christian Asbjornsen was born in Oslo in 1812. As a child, he heard these stories ("eventyr") from people who worked in his father's glazier shop. They came from all parts of Norway to learn how to set glass. On their Sunday hikes through fields and forest, they would take young Peter along and excite his imagination with their stories.

In 1826, Asbjornsen met Jorgen Moe, a farm boy from Ringerike in eastern Norway at Norderhov School. They used every spare moment to hunt, fish, hike and dream of becoming poets.

They got the idea of collecting Norwegian folk stories by reading Grimm's fairy tales from Germany. Their first volume was published in 1845. Jacob Grimm had high praise for their work, saying that the Norwegian folk tales had a freshness and fulness which "surpass nearly all others." They went up and down the valleys listening to stories, especially in Gudbrandsdal and Telemark.

In 1879, an illustrated edition was published with hand drawn pictures by Erik Werenskiold of Kongsvinger. He had studied art both in Oslo and Munich. Later Theodore Kittelson of Kragero joined him as an illustrator. Fortunately, this book, entitled "Norwegian Folk Tales," was re-published in 1982.

In these stories, kings are usually pictured as going around in slippers and smoking long pipes. The clergy, too, were caricatured as being out of touch with the facts of life.

One of my favorite folk tales is called "The Old Woman Against the Stream." These words, "Kjerringa mot strommen," have become a common expression for a stubborn woman. She was so contrary that while arguing with her husband about how to harvest the crop, he drowned her in the river. When she disappeared, he began to think it a pity that she hadn't been given a Christian burial. But alas, her body was nowhere to be found. With the help of friends, he searched everywhere downstream. She had totally disappeared! Then the truth dawned on him. He said, "This old woman of mine had a mind of her own. She was so contrary while she was alive that can't very well be otherwise now. We'll have to start searching upstream." And sure enough, they found that she had floated against the stream and had come to rest above the waterfall! This is genuine Norse humor and everyone would laugh until their insides ached.

As a boy, I enjoyed reading the "Reynard the Fox" stories. I was surprised to find them also in the Asbjornsen-Moe collection. There are a number of troll stories too, including "Billy Goat Gruff."

Many of these tales are common to several European countries and were brought into Norway during the Middle Ages by bards, or storytellers. In the age before television, the storytellers were warmly welcomed into people's homes. Just imagine these stories being told by flickering candlelight in a kitchen with low ceilings during the long winter night or in front of the fireplace. Iverson stated: "The old women usually kept to deep, mystic or eerie themes, while the men related humorous, sometimes bawdy stories."

Another tale that I find amusing is about "The Parson and the Sexton." The parson was an arrogant fellow who would demand the whole road whenever he drove his horse and buggy. His bluff was called one day when he met a man who turned out to be the king. He was ordered to appear in court the next day and be prepared to answer three questions. His job and life depended on the answers.

Not being so good at quizzes, he sent the sexton (a lay assistant) in his place dressed in clergy clothes. The sexton gave very clever answers which satisfied the king. Finally, the king said: "Since you are so wise on all counts, tell me what I'm thinking now!" He replied, "Oh, I suppose you're thinking that it is the parson who's standing here before you. But I'm sorry to say that you're wrong, for it's the sexton." "Aha! Then go home with you, and you be the parson and let him be the sexton," said the king. And so it was.

Are folk stories and fairy tales fit subjects for adult minds? Aren't they meant to tease the imaginations of children? I must admit to losing much of my childhood appreciation for this kind of literature during my years of professional study. But I've changed. I like the inscription written in a well worn book of fairy tales by Hans Christian Andersen in our home. It reads: "Nothing can be truer than fairy wisdom. It is as true as sunbeams." I think, however, that only children and adults who have some of a child's nature in them will be apt to agree.

The Violinist, a woodcarving.

51

CHAPTER 18

John Ericsson And The
Civil War's Great Naval Battle

THE BATTLE OF HAMPTON ROADS in Virginia is remembered as one of the most important naval encounters in history. It cannot, however, be compared to the great battles of Jutland, Midway or the Coral Sea. It was fought by just two strange looking and dissimilar warships. The battle lasted about four hours and the casualties were only a few wounded.

What was the Civil War naval battle all about and why is it remembered? What has it got to do with the Scandinavian heritage?

President Lincoln was pale and visibly shook. Panic was overtaking some of the cabinet members, including Edwin Stanton, Secretary of War. Bad news had come to Washington. For months it had been rumored that the Confederacy was building a fearful new weapon—an ironclad warship!

It was March 8, 1862. Two Union warships, the "Cumberland" and the "Congress," sailed out to stop this dreadful sea monster. Their cannonballs bounced harmless off its slanted iron covered sides which protected its ten cannons. In short order, both Union warships were sunk with much loss of life. President Lincoln's strategy for defeating the South through a naval blockade hung in the balance. If this plan failed, the war could drag on for many years or it might even mean the end of the "United States of America." Secretary Stanton gave a doomsday speech to the President and his colleagues. Every ship and seaport city of the North, he claimed, were in imminent danger of destruction. Both Lincoln and Stanton paced the floor, looking out the window to the Potomac River, as though the dreaded warship were soon to arrive.

One cabin member, Gideon Welles, appeared unruffled by the news. As the Secretary of the Navy, he had a secret. Naval intelligence was well aware of what the "rebs" were doing. Now it was the Navy Secretary's turn to speak. He advised calm since the Confederate warship's size was too deep to sail up the Potomac and it was not seaworthy enough to reach New York. Then he told them that the Union was also building an "ironclad." One of the cabinet members asked: "How many guns does it have?" "Two," replied Welles. Horrified unbelief came over Stanton.

The next day, large crowds gathered to watch the "Merrimac" (renamed the "Virginia") return for battle against the Union fleet. It headed directly to finish off the badly damaged "Minnesota." Out of nowhere a strange looking craft appeared. Some called it a "Yankee cheese box on a raft." The U.S.S. Monitor's two cannons took about seven minutes to prepare for firing each cannonball. Five times the Merrimac rammed the smaller vessel. Its iron frame held. Volleys were exchanged with some damage to both ships. At noon, the Monitor withdrew from battle and the Merrimac was almost out of cannonballs, so it left the Minnesota and sailed off claiming victory. But the North interpreted the news differently. The little Monitor had done its job. The mighty Merrimac had been stopped! Lincoln was ecstatic and the North was jubilant.

The architect of that strange looking and quickly constructed Union craft was John Ericsson. He had been born in Varmland, Sweden, July 13, 1803. Though of irascible temperament, he became famous for his inventive skills by the time he was 13. At age 23, he was honored in London. At 36, he emigrated to America. Among his 2000 inventions was an improved model of the screw propeller which was to power large ships. He died in 1889.

What effect could such a little duel have on history? It marked the beginning of a new age in ship building. In London, the battle was talked about by everyone. As a result, the British built a new ironclad navy. They had experimented with a few models, but the Monitor/Merrimac clash was the clincher. This was also one of the first naval battles fought by two steam powered ships, also one of Ericsson's projects.

It was, I suppose, only proper that a Scandinavian inventor should have made such a contribution to the future navies of the world. Afterall, they had built the "longships."

How did Secretary Welles discover this "classic genius inventor," as historian Page Smith described him? Would you believe, it was a

Harvard professor of pastoral theology named Horace Bushnell who made the introduction? He and Welles had been long time friends.

Don't underestimate the value of old friends. They can turn out to be your greatest asset. Just remember the panic in the president's cabinet and the Swedish inventor who saved the day. And if you visit Stockholm, see for yourself the proud statue the Swedes have erected of Ericsson by the harbor.

CHAPTER 19

"St. Olaf"—
Norway's Best Remembered King

W HEN I FIRST LEARNED the nursery rhyme, "London bridge is falling down," I had no idea that it was about Norway's most famous king. He is best known to us as "St. Olaf" or "Olaf the Holy" (Heilige Olaf). He had other names too: Olaf II, Olaf Haraldsson and Olaf the Stout or Thick. What is the connection between this Olaf and the London bridge? And why has his fame survived?

Olaf Haraldsson, who ruled from 1014-1028, was Norway's second king by that name. The first was Olaf Tryggvason (995-1000). The present king of Norway, Olav V, is descended from this line. The "Olafs" (now spelled "Olav") came from a Swedish royal family called the "Ynglings." They entered Norway shortly before the Viking Age (793-1066). The first king to claim rule over all Norway was an Yngling, Harald Finehair, about 890. Olav V also traces his ancestry to Gorm, the founder of Denmark's royal family who lived about 940.

Olaf Haraldsson's father descended from Harald Finehair, but he died quite young. His mother remarried a farmer-king named Sigurd Syr. Olaf was not a model child, unless one should be thinking of a young "Viking." He was pagan in all his ways and showed little respect for his foster father. He was of average height but was very stout. He had medium brown hair and eyes that no one could face when angry. He also excelled in athletic contests and in oratory.

Olaf was only 12 when he went with an uncle on his first Viking cruise. He was especially hostile to the Swedes because they had killed his father. Olaf's craving for adventure brought him to England and to service under King Ethelred. There he fought against the Danes who controlled London and most of England. During an attack on London, it was his idea to fix grappling hooks on the piers which held up the London bridge. His rowers pulled hard and the bridge collapsed. London, however, remained with the Danes.

With just 120 followers, Olaf invaded Norway in 1014. He had swift success. Many joined him because he had descended from King Harald. His chief opposition came from the large landowners (bønders) who were against a centralized government. But Olaf outwitted them in both battle and diplomacy.

During a stay in Normandy, a part of France settled by Scandinavians, Olaf became a Christian and was baptized. He took his conversion seriously and became a relentless missionary. Charlemagne (d. 814), the Christian emperor of France, was his model for a ruler. Like his hero, Olaf employed non-compromising methods of evangelism. First, he would speak gently to the people, imploring them to leave their idols and to believe in Christ. Then he invited them to be baptized. But he was firm in demanding decision. He warned them that if they refused they had three choices: Go into exile, become slaves or face him in battle. In a short time, Norway became a part of "Christendom." Clergy from England accompanied Olaf to instruct the people.

King Knut (Canute), the Danish ruler of England, forced Olaf into exile with the Viking rulers of Russia in 1028. Two years later, Olaf hastily returned wih a small army to reclaim his kingdom. He expected that people would join him in rising up against the Danes. King Knut, however, made many promises and most of the farmers marched against Olaf.

On July 29, 1030, Olaf met the enemy at Stiklestad, north of Trondheim. By this time, he had changed in many of his ways. He no longer burned the homes of his enemies, as was the custom. He listened to the reading of the Bible and partook of Holy Communion every morning. But on the day of battle, he was greatly outnumbered. The swords began to clash at noon and by three o'clock Olaf lay dead. His friends secretly buried his body in Trondheim, called Nidaros.

Many people claimed that the dead Olaf performed miracles for them. Even those who struck his death blows praised his virtues. Olaf had become a folk hero against the broken promises of King Knut. A year later, Bishop Grimkel examined the corpse of Olaf. When he opened the coffin, "there was a delightful and fresh smell...his cheeks were red...his hair and nails had grown." Live coals did not burn his beard. Both bishop and the "things" (the ruling councils) were convinced that Olaf was "holy." They did not wait for approval from church authorities in Rome. The Norwegians knew a saint when they saw one. His body was moved to the spot where Norway's national cathedral stands today near the Trondheim harbor. This is also where Norway's kings are consecrated today.

A few years ago, I visited with a pastor from Norway. He was interested in my family name because it originates from a valley southwest of Trondheim. He asked: "Did you know that the Fiske farmers fought at Stiklestad?" In surprise, I said, "Really?" "Yes," he replied, "but they fought on the wrong side."

CHAPTER 20

The Saarinens: Finland's
Architectural Gift To America

EVERYONE HAS SOME SPECIAL PLACE that they like to be. One of my favorite spots is on the first base side of home plate in Busch Memorial Stadium in St. Louis. I admit to being an ardent Cardinal baseball fan. But why do I like to sit there? It's so I can look over the rim of the stadium and see the "Arch," the "gateway to the West."

The Arch, of course, is really the Jefferson National Expansion Memorial. It stands 630 feet high and is the same distance at the base between its two giant legs. It is built of reinforced concrete and is covered by ¼ inch thick plates of stainless steel. Constructed between 1962 and 1964, the Arch marks the expansion into western USA through the "Louisiana Purchase." President Thomas Jefferson closed the deal with Emperor Napoleon on May 4, 1803, for $15,000,000. The French needed money for their continental wars.

St. Louis became the point of entry to the West for explorers, fur traders, soldiers, mountain men, missionaries and settlers. The westward movement attracted some unusual people: Meriwether Lewis and William Clark, Jedidiah Smith, Fr. Joseph DeSmet and the Choteaus, just to name a few. Until the railroad was built from Chicago to Sioux City, Iowa, as a shortcut to the Missouri River, almost everyone had to travel through St. Louis.

In 1948, Eero Saarinen (1920-1961) won the competition for the best design for the memorial. President Roosevelt had authorized the planning on Dec. 22, 1935. Today, millions of people have visited the Arch and have been amazed at its design and at the museum which it houses. It's built in the shape of a "catenary curve," the same shape into which a hanging chain will form. Nothing like it had been constructed before and it thrust Eero Saarinen into international recognition.

This was nothing new, however, for the Saarinens. Eero's father, Eliel Saarinen (1873-1950), was already a celebrated architect both in Europe and America. The elder Saarinen was born in Rantasalmi, Finland. Educated at the Polytechnic Institution in Helsinki, he was an advocate of modern and functional design. It was his Finnish Pavilion at the Paris Exposition in 1900 that gave him his international fame. In Finland, he is best remembered for the Helsinki Central Railway Station. In 1923, he emigrated to the US and became a professor of architecture at the University of Michigan. His wife, Loja, was also a distinguished designer. Among his famous American buildings are many schools and churches. He became a US citizen in 1945 and was the author of several books.

There probably has never been a father-son combination so famous in architecture. Eero, the son, was born in Kirkonummi, Finland. He graduated from the Yale School of Architecture in 1934. His most famous project was the Arch. At the top of this memorial monument is a gallery for visitors. It's reached by riding in capsules holding five people which travel like an enclosed aerial ski lift. The Arch was built to withstand winds up to 150 mph.

There are many other designs which also brought Eero Sarinen fame. These include the TWA terminal at Kennedy Airport in New York, as well as the Dulles Airport near Washington, DC, the US embassies in Oslo and London, the hockey rink at Yale University, the Lincoln Center for Performing Arts and the CBS building in New York. Other works of Eero Saarinen which appeal to me are the campus of Concordia Seminary in Ft. Wayne, Indiana, and Christ Lutheran Church in Minneapolis which has influenced the design of many more churches.

Finland is a small country of over 70,000 lakes and less than five million people. A third of its land surface is covered by marshlands and peat bogs. In its 800 years of settlement, the Finns have had an heroic history. Finland was under Swedish rule for almost 600 years (1216-1809) and a little more than 100 years (1809-1917) under Russian. The Finns have had self rule only since Dec. 6, 1917. The world will never forget Finland's courage in resisting the military might of the Soviet Union in the Winter War of 1939-1940. The endurance and imagination of the Finnish character continues to live in over 600,000 people who claim Finland as their ancestral home while citizens of the USA.

In the years that I lived in St. Louis (1961-1967), I don't ever remember meeting a Finn. But the 630 foot tall Arch more than made up for this. It towers above all the structures of the city's new and beautiful riverfront. I hope that my grandsons who share in the Finnish heritage will always be proud of this ethnic connection.

And I, as a latter-day Norseman, will enjoy my favorite chair with its molded plywood frame, which is also a Saarinen creation. Then I'll scan the TV programs for a Cardinal baseball game. Perhaps they will show the Arch one more time.

CHAPTER 21

Danes Solve 2000 Year Old
Murder Mystery

"**P**ROFESSOR GLOB? This is the police. A murdered body has been found. Would you come and take a look at it?"

It was May 8, 1950. Dr. P. V. Glob was professor of European Archaeology at Aarhus University on the east coast of Jutland in Denmark. The murdered body was buried in a peat bog at Tollund, west of Aarhus. The peat was being removed to reclaim the land for farming. The workers had called the police, suspecting a connection with a recent murder.

The police, however, suspected that there may be more than met the eyes of the peat cutters. That is why they called Prof. Glob away from his classroom. Before the sun had set over the hills in that region of central Jutland, the professor and his students were on the scene. There they saw a man as though he were asleep, lying on his right side. He was naked except a skin cap on his head and a belt. There was a leather braided rope around his neck. Examination showed that his skull had been smashed. Who was this stranger buried in an unmarked grave? Why had he been murdered? Who did it and when?

What Prof. Glob learned has turned out to be one of the most scary murder stories in all history. The man had been killed by hanging, yet his facial features were serene. How long had he been there? Would you believe 2000 years? Using the latest in scientific methods for determining dates, both pollen analysis and carbon tests were made. The inner organs (heart, lungs, liver plus both large and small intestines) were in perfect condition. In fact, the victim's last meal has been analyzed as a "gruel," the recipe for which was later used by two English archaeologists. They reported that just to eat this meal was an ordeal. They washed it down with aquavit, a Danish brandy, something which the Tollund man did not have.

This body was only one of almost 1500 which have been unearthed in Europe. About 600 of these have been in Denmark and a few in

Sweden and Norway. Over half have been found in Germany. Most of these burials took place between 100 B.C. and 500 A.D. A few go back as far as 5000 years and some as recent as World War II. The first recorded discovery was in 1640. My father-in-law, who grew up in northern Jutland, told me about hearing of several such finds when he was a boy.

Was there any reason why these "bog people" were buried in the cold peat? What about the Tollund man? Prof. Glob has written that some were criminals and a bog grave was a part of their execution. He pointed out that cowards, shirkers and the very dangerous were so punished to cover up their shame. Suicides and witches may also have been laid in bogs with a wooden stake to pin them to the earth so they would not return to haunt the living.

What about the Tollund man? Prof Glob claimed that he and the majority of such discoveries were human sacrifices. It is believed that he had first been hung as an offering to the gods and then planted in the earth to insure a good harvest for the community.

These early iron age victims were sacrificed to Nerthus, "Mother Earth." Human sacrifice was the price she demanded for her favors at fertility festivals. These were held in the Spring prior to the planting season. The worship of Nerthus began about 500 B.C. in Denmark. It seemed a small price to pay to gain a good harvest.

But why did the Tollund man look like he was actually happy? It could only be that he believed sincerely in his religion. To die in this way was not loss but gain. He would go to be entertained by the goddess and her fair maidens and his family and neighbors would eat for another year. For this he would even endure having his throat slit from ear to ear.

Only the head of the Tollund man has been preserved for posterity. I saw it in the museum at Silkeborg, just six miles from where it was found. It's not pretty, even though the museum is fascinating. It's estimated that he was between 30 and 40 years old.

Imagine the shock to the peat cutters when they discovered that the body they found was not the corpse of a recent murder, but the body of a man sacrificed in religious ritual 2000 years ago. The preservation of bodies in the the cold peat had been so perfect that finger prints have

62

been taken of the victims.

About 300 feet away from the burial site of the Tollund man, the body of a 30 year old woman was found in 1938. Besides human bodies, ceremonial wagons, ships, pottery vessels and even a silver cauldron have been found buried in the peat bogs. These are believed to have been for the use of the victim in the after-world life.

These sacrifices stopped when Christianity came to Denmark. The missionaries persuaded the people that the perfect sacrifice had been made by another Victim.

CHAPTER 22

"Black Death"
Strikes Europe

IT WAS EARLY AUGUST 1349, when an English merchant ship drifted into the Bergen harbor. On board was a cargo of wool from London. Then it ran aground. When the sailors made no effort to free it, the port authorities boarded the vessel to investigate. To their horror, they found the entire crew dead. They realized too late that there was another cargo aboard—"Black Death."

They issued a quarantine, but the plague got ahead of them. As people fled, they carried the disease. In a few months, all of Norway was infected. It soon spread to Sweden, Finland, Denmark and Greenland. It took 53 years to reach Iceland.

The term "Black Death" ("swarta doden" in Swedish) is a bit of a mystery. It was coined 200 years later. An earlier name in Latin, "atra mors," meaning "terrible death," was also used. A chronicler wrote: "It was a disease in which there appeared certain swellings in the groin and under the armpits, and the victims spat blood, and in three days they were dead." Prof. Robert S. Gottfried of Rutgers University has written a book entitled, "The Black Death: Natural and Human Disaster in Medieval Europe." He claims that "Black Death should be ranked as the greatest biological-environmental event in history, and one of the turning points of Western Civilization."

What was the Black Death? Where did it originate and why couldn't medical skills resist it? Black Death, now called "Yersinia pestis," first appeared in the Gobi Desert in central Asia in the 1320s. It followed the trade routes which carried silk and spices, entering Sicily in October 1347. According to Gottfried, it was "a combination of bubonic, pneumonic and septicaemic plague strains." It was a tiny bacillus that lived in the stomach of a flea carried by rats. In just four years, 1347-1351, it killed between 17 and 28 million people in Europe. Rats were common in those times of poor public health. No one seems to have suspected the role of the rodent in the spread of the disease. In colder climates, like Scandinavia, the infection went into the lungs and caused severe coughing, spitting of blood, nervous disorders, coma and death.

The medical books dealing with plagues were over 1000 years old and had no "germ theory." In fact, it was not until the early part of the 20th century that the disease was identified. Once established, the plague continues in cycles for centuries. In 1986, it killed thousands of gophers in western North Dakota.

Massive population loss resulted from the plague. Up to two-thirds of the people in some areas of Norway died. It was especially hard on clergy and physicians as they were required to attend the sick. Large areas of land returned to forest. There is the story of a hunter, many generations later, whose stray arrow struck a church bell hidden in the forest. Inside, he found a bear hibernating in front of the altar.

Before the plagues, farm land was in danger of overuse and wild animals were found only in the far north. But it was not long before wolves were seen in the suburbs of Paris. The economy suffered from low prices and high labor costs.

Religious fanaticism reared its head. First, bands of "flagellants" roamed Europe promising deliverance through their self-inflicted sufferings. They cut and beat themselves in religious ritual, believing that they were appeasing the wrath of God against the sins of the world. Second, mass hysteria and panic sought scapegoats. In the Moslem Middle East it was the Christians, in the West it was the Jews and in Spain it was the Arabs. Like the days of Hitler, a "holocaust" took a great toll of lives.

If any good came out of this evil, it was the new beginnings in medical care. Physicians turned away from their ancient theories which favored "blood letting" as therapy. Hospitals became places to heal people rather than isolating the sick until they died. The feudal system of lords and serfs was also broken.

A few years ago, I visited a small log cabin near Hattfjelldal, about 250 miles north of Trondheim. It dated from 1823 and was the first Norwegian home built in that area after the Black Death. Imagine, this valley had been desolate of Norsemen for 474 years! Wild animals and Lapps with their reindeer had moved into the region.

THE SCANDINAVIAN HERITAGE

The human race has a remarkable record of survival. We now know how to control the bubonic plague. But new dangers threaten human life today. Are we willing to deal with the ills of human behavior such as poverty, greed and injustice like we attacked the bacillus in the stomach of the rat flea? Will we do it before a new "Black Death" is unleashed. I believe it's worth trying.

CHAPTER 23

John Hanson—
America's First President

ALMOST EVERYONE IN THE WHOLE WORLD knows that George Washington was the first president of the United States. This was one of the first things I learned at school. Why then should this claim be made for someone else? And who was this "John Hanson" anyway? I never read about him in school books. Did he really exist?

Between Annapolis, Maryland and the District of Columbia, there is a four lane highway named for John Hanson. The U.S. Postal Service has issued a stamp with his picture. I also found some unused six cent postcards in a desk drawer with his picture and inscription "John Hanson—Patriot." So he must have existed.

John Hanson was a fourth generation Swedish-American born April 3, 1721, in Maryland. Jacob A. Nelson, a lawyer from Decorah, Iowa, wrote a book on Hanson in 1939. He admitted that information on this early American was hard to find, but that it is verifiable.

According to Nelson, the Hanson ancestry can be traced to Yorkshire, England, in the middle of the 13th century. That was where the Danes had their kingdom a few centuries earlier. The name was changed to Hanson, meaning "son of Henry," about 1340. The Hansons moved to Sweden and intermarried with the royal family. A Colonel John Hanson was killed in the battle of Lutzen, Nov. 16, 1632, defending King Gustavus Adolphus. The king also died that same day. In 1642, Queen Christina sent four of Hanson's sons to Maryland to join the Swedish settlers on the banks of the Delaware River. The colony, known as "New Sweden," had been founded in 1638. In her book, "Finns in North America," Eloise Engle notes that a part of Hanson's ancestry goes back to Swedes who lived in Finland. At that time, Finland was governed by Sweden. Later on the Dutch and then the English took control of Maryland.

The Hansons were highly ambitious and capable colonists. They were active in government and were successful farmers. Samuel Hanson, John's father, was a member of the Maryland General Assembly, a sheriff and held other offices.

The Hanson home had an air of aristocracy about it. Yet they were well liked by their neighbors for their honesty and patriotism. Patriotism, of course, meant loyalty to King George of England. They were also known for their piety. Every day they gathered for Bible reading and prayer. By the time John was 12, he had memorized long sections of the Bible, the catechism and many hymns. There is a tradition that young John was educated at Oxford University in England.

After marriage and settling down with his family, John became active in Maryland politics. Though loyal to British rule, he sided with the colonists in the grievances against the mother country. He was strongly opposed to the "Stamp Act Congress" that met in New York. Among his close acquaintances were Ben Franklin, Thomas Jefferson, the Adams' and other early colonial leaders. After the British reprisals against the people of Boston for the "Tea Party," Hanson sent a substantial gift of silver for the relief of the people.

Hanson was a leader in the independence movement of the colonies. When the Continental Congress was formed, he became the first president. On a memorial plaque at the Frederick County Court House in Maryland, he is remembered as "President of the United States in Congress Assembled, Nov. 5, 1781 to Nov. 4, 1782," and as a signer of the Articles of Confederation.

George Washington sent President Hanson a letter of congratulations and promised him his loyalty in leading the new government. He signed the letter: "Your most obedient servant, George Washington." Hanson's confidence in Washington was also unqualified. He wrote: "We will win the war with George Washington in the field, if we do our share at home. In the end we will establish an Inseparable Union, and ultimately it will become the greatest nation in the world." Two of his sons gave their lives for the cause of this freedom.

If you visit Washington, D.C., you can find John Hanson's statue in the capitol building. Pause a moment before it and remember the Swedish-American boy who grew up to give so much for his country.

CHAPTER 24

The Day The Nazis
Lost Denmark

I T TAKES A LOT OF COURAGE and diplomacy for the little folks to survive on the playground with a big bully running wild. That's the situation in which the Danes found themselves when the Nazis occupied their land on April 9, 1940. It was a long nightmare—49 months of cruel oppression. But Aug. 29, 1943, is marked forever in Danish memory as the day its people defied Hitler's war machine and ended the efforts to bring the Danes into the "New Order." This was the day that the Nazis "lost" Denmark. They continued to occupy it until May 4, 1945, but the charade was over.

Denmark has often been criticized for its passive resistance to the enemy. There were, however, those Danes who wanted "Norwegian conditions" of active resistance. But Denmark is different. There are few natural places to hide. Norway's mountains offered many hideouts into which Nazis did not dare to travel. The only place to hide in Denmark was in homes or through flight to Sweden.

Winston Churchill, England's Prime Minister, had stated that Denmark could not expect help from England if Hitler attacked. As in the days of Napoleon, most people expected the land armies would triumph over Britain's navy. Many prominent Americans urged England to make any kind of peace possible with the Nazis. So you can hardly blame the Danes if they tried to play it "cool."

There were many "apocryphal" stories about the role of Denmark's King Christian X in his defiance of the enemy. Even though these may not all have historical substance, they were useful for national morale. One amusing story had to do with a successful British air raid on the rail yards at Fredrikshavn in northern Jutland. The Nazis ordered the Danish newspapers to report that the bombs fell harmlessly in a pasture, killing a cow. Two days later, the press reported that "the cow that was killed in the R.A.F. raid two days ago is still burning." The Danes found ridicule the best way to deal with a bully.

THE SCANDINAVIAN HERITAGE

There were a few collaborators in Denmark and a very small Nazi party. There was a small "Frikorps Danmark" that was recruited to fight on the Russian front. The Communists were a small but highly organized part of the Resistance movement. They took their orders, however, from Moscow and did not become active in the Resistance until after Hitler invaded Russia in June 1941.

The underground Resistance movement was difficult to organize. The Gestapo was everywhere and ruthlessly suppressed opposition by torture and bribery. Even today, 40 years after the war has ended, some members of the underground living in Denmark are still reluctant to talk about their activities. There still seems to be some fear of possible Nazi reprisals. It may take many years for most of the truth to surface.

In the Spring of 1943, London sent word that the Danes would have to step up their sabotage or the British bombers would level factories producing war materials for the Nazis. This would mean increased Danish casualties. The Danish response took the Nazis by surprise. Dr. Werner Best, in charge of the occupation, was sure that he had charmed the King and his Cabinet into total cooperation. Denmark was regarded as Hitler's "caged canary." In January 1943, only 16 acts of sabotage were committed. By August, it had risen to 220. Saboteurs were trained in England and dropped by parachute into Denmark. Radio London gave coded messages to reception groups.

The Danes became very daring. They blew up factories in broad daylight. Strikes spread throughout the country. Jealousies within the enemy's occupation forces undermined Dr. Best's hope to stay in favor with Berlin.

The Nazis demanded that the Danes completely capitulate to Hitler's demands. Curfew, the death penalty and prohibition of public gatherings did not stop the strikes. Martial law was declared. Danish police were arrested by the Nazis. The Danish Army and Navy were dismantled, but not before half of the fleet was scuttled.

King Christian X, though virtually a prisoner, never lost his courage or his sense of humor. He was the symbol that kept hope alive in those difficult days. He could be a master of sarcasm when it was needed.

During his daily horseback ride through the city, he never returned the salutes from the occupying officers.

Though the Nazis held the guns and had their way, their hold over the Danish spirit was broken. They gave up their attempts to "convert" Denmark's soul. One of the most thorough studies of this period is a three volume work by Jorgen Haestrup entitled "Secret Alliance."

As Aug. 23, 1943, drew to a close, Dr. Best called a meeting of the Danish newspaper men and blamed them for his failure of administration. He said: "The press has implanted the belief that Hitler is weak." Even bullies want someone to like them.

CHAPTER 25

Where Did The Greenlanders Go?

MANY IMPORTANT EVENTS have had strange beginnings and even stranger endings. The Norse colonization in Greenland is such a story.

Erik the Red, father of Leif the Lucky, was banished from Iceland in 982 for three years for being too hasty with the sword. He made a hurried exit with his family and possessions to Greenland and became its chieftain. It was ideally suited for farming, fishing and hunting. When his exile was over, Erik returned to Iceland where plenty of volunteers were ready to go with him to settle this new land.

Three hundred immigrants set sail in 25 ships with livestock and personal possessions. Only 14 ships arrived. They settled in two areas on the west coast of this large island (840,000 square miles). Two settlements were developed: Julianehaab, near the southern tip; and Godthaab, to the north, which is the present capital. More people followed. Danish archaeologists have found about 330 Norse farm sites. It is estimated that about 3000 people may have lived there. The climate was warmer in those days and there were actually a few green places in that frozen land. Today, people find it hard to believe that it should be called "Greenland." I have flown over this island. From 40,000 feet, it looks like a solid chunk of ice and snow. Historical records show that it was misrepresented to attract settlers. The Icelanders were eager to find free land and Leif was a good real estate salesman.

For almost 300 years (984-1261), Greenland was an independent Norse nation. Then it came under the rule of Norway's kings. In 1126, a bishop arrived from Norway to look after the churches. Each year a shipload of supplies came from Bergen. But in 1350, travel between the two lands dropped sharply. The Black Death of 1349 and colder weather patterns isolated these western Norsemen. The last supply boat arrived in 1410. An occasional English boat also stopped. When King Christian IV (1588-1648) sent an expedition to Greenland in the early 1600's, no trace was found of the old colonies. It was not unil 1721 that a new Scandinavian colonization took place, this time from Denmark. Eskimoes told Missionary Hans Egede that the Norsemen "had gone away."

Where did the Greenlanders go? Nobody knows for sure. The Black Death, battles with the Skraelings (Eskimoes), starvation and death at sea have been suggested. But by the time Columbus rediscovered America, there was no more contact with the Greenlanders.

In 1944, Reider T. Sherwin, a native of Norway, published a study entitled "The Old Norse Origin of the Algonquin Language" in five volumes. Volume I has 161 pages of word studies comparing the Old Norse with the Algonquin dialects in northeastern USA and eastern Canada. Having examined his research, I am fascinated by his idea that some of the Greenlanders may have gone to the New World and mingled their language and blood with the earlier Americans. One of the words which is the same in both tongues is "vik." It means a "bay," "inlet" or a "creek." It is the very word from which we get "Viking."

Olaf Norlie, formerly a professor at St. Olaf College, was one of those who favored the "Algonquin" theory. Early explorers in Canada and even in South America report having seen blonde and blue eyed Indians. Over 1000 Old Norse words have been found in the Indian languages in the state of Washington.

One of the tribes which spoke an Algonquin dialect was the Potawatomi of eastern Wisconsin. They were neighbors to the first Norse settlers in the Badger state during the 1840s. This was a settlement of people who had come from Drammen, Norway, to Muskego, about 25 miles southwest of Milwaukee in Racine County. The Norse spoke well of their "Red" neighbors and regarded them as hospitable, peace loving and trustworthy.

On the site of the first Norwegian church built in Norway township on "Indian Hill," there is a sign which reads "Velkommen" ("Welcome"). If we should ever find out that the Potawatomi tribe erected this sign to welcome the immigrants, we might have an interesting clue about what happened to the Greenlanders. However, "Old Norse" and modern Norwegian have many differences.

Knowing what determined people the descendants of Erik the Red were, I can't believe that they would just sit around and freeze to death. They knew about "Vinland" and probably decided to find the hytte (cottage) that Leif Erikson had built some 400 years before and feast on Vinland's famed grapes.

CHAPTER 26

Hans Heg—
Hero Of Chickamauga

H ANS WAS ONLY ELEVEN when his family caught "America Fever." His father, Even Heg, and his mother, Siri, were packing their belongings to leave for America. They left their home at Lier, near Drammen, Norway, in 1840 for the New World.

Born Dec. 21, 1829, Hans was soon noticed as an unusually bright boy. He was liked by everyone because of his cheerfulness and patience. In later years, this would make him a leader of men. His father was an inn keeper and knew printing. The Hegs did not go to America because of poverty as so many others did. They had money enough when they left Telemark both to buy land and put up buildings.

Following the usual route from New York, they travelled to Buffalo by river and canal. From there they went to Milwaukee by a Great Lakes steamer. Their destination, Muskego, was only 20 miles to the southwest, a day's journey. There they joined settlers who had come a year earlier.

When Hans was 13, his father built a barn that was to become famous as a shelter for immigrants moving westward. It was also a social center, a church and a hospital. Famous pioneer preachers, such Elling Eielsen, the Haugean evangelist, and Claus Clausen, the Danish schoolteacher, came to the community.

The Norwegians at Muskego held hard views on alcohol. The first Norwegian Temperance Society was organized in the Heg Home in 1848. Hans became secretary and his father the president. Pastor Clausen was often invited to stay at their house. During these years, three dreadful cholera outbreaks occurred. Still the people kept faith with their choice of the New World.

Hans was always on the go. He joined the "forty-niners" in search of California gold. Just when he was doing well, word came that his father died. He returned home to take care of the family farm.

But farming couldn't hold him. Hans had a strong social conscience and became active in the politics of Norway Township and Racine County. He believed strongly in freedom, equality and brotherhood. As a member of the Wisconsin State Prison Board, he did much to improve conditions in the jails and rehabilitation work.

When the Civil War broke out in 1861, Governor Randall appointed Hans a colonel with authority to recruit Scandinavians for the Fifteenth Wisconsin Volunteers. The Irish and the Germans were also doing this. He advertised for recruits, saying: "The government of our adopted country is in danger. It is our duty as brave and intelligent citizens to extend our hands in defense of our country and of our homes." Eight hundred and ninety enrolled, of whom 115 answered roll to the name "Ole." Pastor Clauson became the chaplain and Dr. S. O. Himoe of the community went as the surgeon.

The regiment had only 16 days of training before going to the Southern front. They fought in 25 battles and skirmishes. The battle for which Heg is best known was at Chickamauga, in northeast Georgia, fought Sept. 19-20, 1863. The Union forces were larger but had unwisely divided themselves as they travelled and were ambushed. It turned out to be one of the worst defeats of the Union in the whole war. Heg's men were given difficult ground. They held fast and counter-attacked repeatedly. Heg was everywhere. He wouldn't order a soldier to go anywhere that he was unwilling to go.

About sunset on the first day, a Confederate sharpshooter shot Hans in the bowels. He continued on horseback to direct the attack and refused medical aid. Finally, loss of blood forced him to turn over his command to Lt. Col. Ole C. Johnson. He died the next day at noon. When the Union commander, "Rosey" Rosecrans received the news, he wrote: "I am sorry to hear that Heg has fallen. He was a brave officer, and I intended to promote him to be general." Heg was the highest ranking Union officer from Wisconsin to die in the war.

Heg's grave is located close to Norway Lutheran Church on Indian Hill, about 25 miles northwest of Racine. Across the highway is a state park with a museum named for him. There is a statue of Heg with a commanding presence by the park.

Heg had learned English well and I think it quite possible that he might have become the first Scandinavian born governor in the USA, had not war struck him down. Theodore C. Blegen paid Heg this tribute: "The valorous blood of the old Vikings ran in his veins, united with the gentler virtues of a Christian gentleman."

One hundred and twenty years after Chickamauga, I stood in silence before his grave, full of thought. He was only 33. He really loved this land. How often had his wife and children stood there too?

CHAPTER 27

The Vikings
In France

THE VIKINGS DIDN'T NEED an invitation to go visiting. They were experts in detecting weaknesses in their neighbor's defences. By the year 800, they had invaded Germany, but were careful to avoid direct contact with France so long as Charlemagne was emperor. After his death in 1814, they tested out the toughness of his sons. Soon their longships were raiding the coastlands and probing the interior.

By 841, they plundered Rouen and advanced on Paris. In another four years, they destroyed Hamburg and moved about Germany as they pleased. The Vikings were not only seen as plundering savages, but as wild eyed heathen who had no respect for life. They got their kicks by torturing enemy prisoners. (This was not unique to the Vikings.) It was in those days that this prayer was supposed to have been lifted up in the churches of France: "From the fury of the Northmen, O Lord, deliver us."

There was a handsome boy born to an earl of the Orkney Islands. His father had once been a powerful ruler in Norway and was a friend of King Harald Haarfager. He was so large that no horse (actually, fjord ponies) could hold him, so he had to walk wherever he wanted to go. He was known as "Ganger Rolf," or "Rolf the Walker." Most history books call him "Rollo." He made the mistake of stealing some of King Harald's cattle (a perfectly normal thing for a Viking to do) as he camped in Norway. It made the King so angry that he outlawed Rolf from the land.

From his exile in the Hebrides off the coast of Scotland, Rolf practised his raiding skills on England. Then he turned to France. All went well until the battle of Chartres in 911. The Vikings took a severe beating. The French King, Charles II, sighing relief, offered Rolf a treaty that would permit the Vikings to keep the land which they already occupied. They met in a small chapel at St. Clair-sur-Epte. There were two conditions. First, the Norsemen must swear loyalty to the French king and keep newly arrived Vikings from attacking Paris and other French cities. Second, they must be baptized and become Christian. The French always insisted on conversion as part of a treaty with pagans. To decline was suicide.

The ceremony of allegiance required Rolf to kiss the royal foot. Legend tells us that Rolf picked up the king's leg and lifted it straight into the air to his mouth. The king fell helplessly on his back while Rolf's warriors roared with laughter. They must have been quite a scene in chapel.

But for all that Rolf (Robert I, as the English called him), kept his bargain, including conversion to the Christian faith. That area of northwest France is called Normandy ("Northmandy"), which means "dukedom of the Norsemen." Many more Scandinavians came from both Denmark and Norway. To this day, blue eyes and blond hair set Normandy off from the rest of France.

The Norsemen proved to be expert organizers of government and became leaders in law, education and in the church. They also became "French" in language and customs. That has been characteristic of Scandinavians. They quickly integrated into the local population (except Ireland). The same was true in America. It has been only in the last century that there has been much attempt to preserve the Scandinavian heritage in the New World.

A descendant of Rolf, named William the "Bastard," became obsessed with his rights to the English throne. He took advantage of the English heir, Harald Godwinson, when he was shipwrecked off the coast of France. Treating him with great honor, he exacted a promise of loyalty from him. But it was a trick. As soon as the oath was made, the cover was taken off the table and it revealed sacred relics. This made the oath binding.

The English prince, also a Viking descendant, returned home to rule. But it was not long before William crossed the channel with an army. Harald, weakened from having fought a fierce battle with the Norwegian King Harald Hardraada near York, rallied his tired troops to face the well rested Normans. They met at Hastings on Oct. 14, 1066, a landmark day in English history. Harald was killed and William became known as the "Conqueror." The whole story of William and Harald is reserved on a tapesty in the Archbishop's palace at Bayeux, Normandy.

The Normans ("Northmen") completely changed England. They introduced the feudal system of land ownership with its lords and manors. Ireland was conquered. But its permanent effect on us is what it did to the English language. It blended Old Norse, Celtic, French and Church Latin. So if spelling English words is your downfall, blame it on the Normans, those Vikings in France.

CHAPTER 28

Norway's
Royal Family

NORWAY'S ROYAL FAMILY was well known to me as a boy growing up on a North Dakota farm. A large picture of King Haakon VII and Queen Maud, together with the ministers of state and the Domkirken (cathedral) in Trondheim, dominated our living room wall. Only later did I learn about George Washington and Abraham Lincoln. The picture now hangs in my house as a reminder to our children and grandchildren of their heritage.

It was Nov. 25, 1905, when the new king and his family arrived in Oslo to begin a reign of almost 52 years. Just a week before, the Storting (parliament) had elected Denmark's Prince Karl to be the first real king of Norway in 525 years. Ninety-one years of rule by Swedish kings ended in a political impasse. Oscar II gave up his claim to Norway in frustration.

It was not a foregone conclusion that the new Norwegian Government would be a monarchy. Many leaders had "republican" sympathies and wanted a president. Two reasons prevailed to elect a king. First, it was tradition in Norway to have royalty. Second, most of Norway's neighbors had kings and this would make for peaceful borders.

Prince Karl took the name of Haakon VII. Haakon VI (1350-1380) had been Norway's last "Norwegian" king. When he died, his Danish born queen, Margaret I, controlled the government until her death in 1412.

The new king brought the world's oldest royal family line to Norway. King Haakon had descended from Denmark's King Gorm (died about 940). The earlier Norse kings had descended from the Swedish "Yngling" family. They appear to have been driven out of Sweden and moved to Norway in search of a land to rule.

The new queen, Maud, was the daughter of England's King Edward VII. He did some political arm twisting to influence Norway's decision.

Their son, Alexander, was renamed "Olav." Since he was just two years old, he would be reared as a genuine Norwegian. This remembrance of Norway's "saint" king was a good sign for the future. Their royal motto is "Alt for Norge" ("Everything for Norway). They have kept their promise.

The new king was dearly loved and many Norwegian-Americans began to name their sons "Haakon," just as they had previously named them "Oscar." During World War II, he worked courageously in England for Norway's freedom.

Crown Prince Olav and his Swedish wife, Crown Princess Martha, were very popular both in Norway and America. She was the great, great granddaughter of King Karl Johan of the French Bernadotte family who had come to Sweden as Crown Prince in 1810. Karl Johan's statue stands in front of the palace in Oslo. In their 1939 tour of America, Olav and Martha were greeted by large crowds of admirers whose respect and enthusiasm was worthy of envy by any president or governor.

When Olav became king in 1958, there could have been a question whether he should be called Olav V or VI. Prof. Karen Larson of St. Olaf College published "A History of Norway" in 1948 in which she had already listed five Olaf's as kings of Norway. When the announcement was made, however, it was as Olav V. The Olaf listed as king by Prof. Larson from 1103-1116 has lost his place in history. (The reader should be informed that the letters "f" and "v" are interchangeable in phonetic spelling. Modern Norwegian prefers "v" to "f" in proper names. The royal name was "Olaf" in ancient times, but "Olav" today.)

Olav and Martha had three children: Princess Ragnhild, born in 1930; Princess Astrid, born in 1932; and Crown Prince Harald, born in 1937. During World War II, Crown Princess Martha and her children were in America, spending a great deal of time with the Roosevelts at their home in Hyde Park, N.Y. When she died in 1954, Eleanor Roosevelt wrote to the palace in Oslo: "We in this country will not forget Princess Martha. She will always mean to us the finest qualities that a woman can have—courage, patience, kindness and generosity."

Crown Prince Harald has been an able understudy of his father, preparing for the day when he will have to become the head of state. Like King Olav V, he is also a sports enthusiast. Crown Princess Sonja has become very popular in the United States from a recent visit.

Midwestern USA was favored with a visit by Prince Astrid (Mrs. Johan Martin Ferner) at the Norsk Høstfest in Minot, N.D., Oct. 21-23, 1983. Her visit was to honor the children of Norwegian immigrants who, while loyal Americans, have never lost their deep feelings for the land of their heritage. I watched as the Princess was presented to the audience. There was a hushed silence and emotions ran high. I saw many tears of excitement stream down faces in that crowd of thousands.

Princess Astrid is the mother of five children and lives in Oslo. Since her mother died, she has often accompanied the King on visits throughout Norway. She came to the Høstfest as his personal representative. Long live the King, his royal family and their motto: "Alt for Norge."

CHAPTER 29

"Høstfest"—
A Time For Celebration

"HØSTFEST" MEANS "FALL FESTIVAL" and is associated with the end of harvest. It is an ancient custom common to many lands. The Israelites annually celebrated three harvest festivals. The first was during the barley harvest in April. It took on a religious character known as "Passover." Seven weeks later when the wheat was gathered, they observed "Pentecost." The final festival came late in October when the fruit had been picked. It was called the "Feast of Tabernacles" or "Booths," as they pitched tents in the fields.

It is not surprising then that the Scandinavians also had festive gatherings when harvest was completed. Since the days of St. Olaf (d. 1030), Norway and its Nordic neighbors have had special prayers of thanksgiving for harvest time. This stands in stark contrast to the human sacrifices connected with their earlier pagan times.

The special prayer for Høstfest used in Norway during the immigration days began: "Almaegtige Gud, vor naadige Fader, du som oplater din haand og maetter alt levende med gode ting." Translated, this reads: "Almighty God, most merciful Father, who openest thy hand and satisfiest the desire of every living thing." It goes on to pray "for the living seed of Thy word sown in our hearts."

There are many Scandinavian festivals in America today. Among the best known are the Nordic Fest in Decorah, Iowa, and the Nordland Fest in Sioux Falls, South Dakota. The Scandinavian Day Picnic held at Vasa Park near Chicago is one of the newest. Some of the other areas where such gatherings are held include: Seattle, Washington; Detroit, Michigan; Topsfield, Maine; Solvang, California; and Spring Grove, Minnesota.

The Norsk Høstfest celebration in Minot, North Dakota, is unique. It began in 1978 and is held annually at the North Dakota State Fairgrounds. To the overwhelming surprise of the planners, over 5000 people attended the first year even though there had been only seven weeks time from the first committee meeting to the celebration.

It wasn't long before it was the fourth largest event in the state. In 1986, about 35,000 people celebrated Høstfest in Minot. The three larger events last over a week in contrast to the Høstfest's three days.

For the first Høstfest, local talent was recruited for entertainment. But within a short time, musicians even came from Norway and Sweden. A favorite at the event has been Myron Floren, said to be America's most popular accordionist. He quickly captivates the crowds with his easy stage manners and a few Norwegian words. The Minot Høstfest is held in the latter part of October, hopefully before the wintry winds begin to blow and when the farmers are done in the fields. Some of the America's most popular entertainers have appeared at the Høstfest. These include Victor Borge, Burl Ives, Ray Price, Red Skelton, Mel Tillis and Johnny Cash.

Not only has this Høstfest become the "premier Scandinavian event in North America, "as Chicago's Vinland newspaper described it, but it has received recognition in the highest circles of Norway. From the royal family down to the common people, the Høstfest has gotten attention.

To put on a celebration like this takes the skills and dedication of over 600 volunteers. Nothing but the weather can be left to chance. "Snow insurance" is a consideration to cover weather uncertainties. Among the many who have played key parts in this event, one person has provided the leadership that has made this event such a magnificent occasion. Chester Reiten, the president of a CBS affiliated radio and television broadcasting company, who is also a state senator and was for 14 years the mayor of Minot, has been president of the Norsk Høstfest Association since its beginning. He has made several trips to build ties between Minot and Skien, Norway, a city of similar size in Telemark. Each year, official visitors and friends travel between the cities with cultural exchange and to attend each other's celebrations. The Concert Choir of Minot State College has performed in the Skien church.

Visitors to the Høstfest come from all parts of the United States and western Canada. Many wear their "bunads" (local costume dress). There is a queen contest, arts and crafts display, gift shops, food booths and musical entertainment. The Scandinavian-American Hall of Fame was established in 1984. It has inducted such famous persons as Col. Knut Haukelid, World War II Norwegian war hero; Orion Samuelson from WGN radio and television in Chicago; Carl Ben Eielson, famed Arctic aviator from Hatton, North Dakota; Brynhild Haugland of Minot who is the dean of state legislators in the USA; Jan Stenerud of football fame and Nobel Peace Prize winner Norman Borlaug. One of the most stirring moments at the Høstfest is when the flags of each Scandinavian country plus the United States and Canada are presented and the national anthems sung.

Yvonne Ryding, Miss Sweden, was present as "Miss Universe" in 1984 and Hofi Karlsdottir, of Iceland, as "Miss World" in 1986. The "Hjemkomst," the Viking ship which crossed the Atlantic in 1983, has been displayed. A Norwegian worship service ("Høimessegudstjeneste"), using the litury of the immigrants at the beginning of the 20th century, is held as the closing event on Sunday. The sermon in recent years has been in English since the third and fourth generations no longer speak or understand the Norwegian language well enough. Out of this ethnic celebration, the children of immigrants find resources of strength for their loyalty to the New World.

CHAPTER 30

Carl Ben Eielson:
"Viking In The Sky"

THEY CALLED HIM BEN, but he was a "Viking in the Sky." Carl Benjamin Eielson was born July 20, 1897, in Hatton, one of North Dakota's most solid Scandinavian communities.

Ben's father operated a family store in which the future Arctic hero often clerked. Those country stores sold everything a family needed: groceries, clothing, hardware, toys and even salt blocks for the livestock. They also bought eggs and cream from the farmers. But Ben's heart wasn't in the store. It was in the out of doors where he could hunt, swim and go hiking in the woods. In school, Ben was a true scholar and he excelled in debating and sports.

After high school, Ben went off to study law, first at the University of North Dakota in nearby Grand Forks, and later at the University of Wisconsin. In 1929, both schools selected him as one of their most famous alumni. While at Wisconsin, he enlisted in the air service of the US Army on Jan. 17, 1917. After completing his training, he became a Second Lieutenant (later he beame a Colonel). But the war ended and instead of going to France, he went back to Hatton. There he did more clerking and helped to organize an American Legion post.

Flying became Ben's passion. He organized a flying club and went into a partnership to buy a single engine Curtis plane for $2585. He had found his love—stunt flying and giving rides at county fairs. It went pretty well until he hit an air pocket and the plane lost a wing to a telephone line.

Having received his university degree, Ben enrolled at Georgetown University in Washington, D.C., to become serious about law again. People growing up today may not see anything so unusual about this, but back in the 1920s this was not typical. Most North Dakotans at that time did not even get a high school diploma, not to mention a college degree or attend graduate school.

While in Washington, Ben met a congressman from Alaska who

offered him a job as high school principal in Fairbanks. No sooner was he there than he took to flying again. The Yukon Indians were so amazed at Ben that they called him a "Moose Ptarmigan," a grouse with feathered feet that habitated on a moose. On Feb. 21, 1924, Ben made history by flying 500 pounds of mail over 300 miles. It took about five hours instead of the usual month by dog sled. Ben also developed a new type of ski for heavy planes.

Ben was a "pro" and in demand by the best in the business. Wilhjalmur Steffanson, a famous Icelandic-American explorer of the polar regions, wanted Ben to work for him. On one such trip, he was forced down on an ice flow and had to walk over 100 miles to safety. It took 18 days. He was also the first to fly over the North Pole.

In 1928, Ben was an international hero and was honored wherever he travelled. He had not forgotten Hatton, however, and his hometown friends had not forgotten him. On July 21, 1928, they gave him one of the biggest welcomes ever held in the state.

Ben was born for flying and there was no stopping him now. He also made aviation history in Antarctica, covering over 1200 miles that had not been previously mapped.

Then came the final flight. A ship was frozen off the coast of Siberia. Ben and his mechanic, Earl Borland, responded. One rescue attempt was successful. A second was never completed. Ben was lost on Nov. 9, 1929, in a storm. It was suspected that the altimeter was defective. It took over two and a half months to find the wreckage. On March 24, 1930, Hatton and the whole state paid tribute to Ben in the largest funeral in North Dakota's history. Over 10,000 people crowded into the little city. Memorial services were held in other cities too. Schools closed as all eyes focused on St. John's Lutheran Church where the family held membership.

Is Ben forgotten? Not in Hatton. His childhood home has now become a Registered Landmark Historical Site and museum to honor him. It's an impressive building on the outside and the inside reveals woodworking craftsmanship that's difficult to find today. Pictures of Ben and other memorabilia reveal the high estimate in which this young Halling was held by famous people of his day.

Ben is also remembered at the state's Heritage Museum in Bismarck. His artifacts have been displayed at the Norsk Høstfest in Minot and Ben was inducted into the Høstfest's Scandinavian-American Hall of Fame in 1984. He is also remembered in Alaska at the Strategic Air Command's Eielson Air Force Base and by Mt. Eielson, near Mt. McKinley.

There will be more honors for Ben. Heroes like this "Viking in the Sky" will never die in the memories of people whose ethnic pride is just beginning to bloom.

Carl Ben Eielson.

89

CHAPTER 31

Knut—The Dane
Who Ruled England

ONE DAY KING KNUT ("Canute," as the English call him), ordered his throne carried to the seashore when the tide was out. It was near Chichester on the south coast of England. Then the king took his place on the royal chair and commanded his officers and courtiers to stand at attention before him.

As the tide rolled in, King Knut spoke to the rising waters: "You are within my jurisdiction, and the land on which I sit is mine; no one has ever resisted my command with impunity. I therefore command you not to rise over my land and not to presume to wet the clothes or limbs of your Lord." But the water kept rising and soon, king, throne and royal attendants retreated to higher ground.

What kind of madness would possess a king to utter such a command? Had power crazed his mind? No such thing. Back on dry ground, King Knut addressed the people: "Be it known to all inhabitants of the world that the power of kings is empty and superficial, and that no one is worthy of the name king except for Him whose will is obeyed by heaven, earth and sea in accordance with His eternal laws." Then he took off his crown of gold and never wore it again.

Who was this Knut? He was the great grandson of Gorm, the founder of Denmark's royal family. It is the oldest monarchy in the world with its heirs also on the thrones of Norway and England today. It was Knut's grandfather, Harald "Bluetooth," who converted to Christianity and began a royal line of faith which has been unbroken for 1000 years. Knut's father, Svein, conquered England but died only five years later on Feb. 3, 1014.

Knut became England's king on Nov. 30, 1016. He brought peace to a torn nation and was a champion of justice and the rights of the people. The English still call him "Great," a title reserved for only a few rulers in the world's history. The only thing they held against him was that he was "Danish" and not "English," but they came to respect and love him dearly. His rule was firm and he promoted the church's mission. These were happy days for the ancient island.

King Knut, however, was no friend of Norway's King Olaf Haraldsson, later called the "saint." He drove Olaf into a Russian exile and declared himself king of Norway. At the Battle of Sticklestad on July 30, 1030, Olaf's army was crushed by the much larger force of Knut and Olaf died, though perhaps by Norwegian hands. Now Knut was "lord of the whole of Denmark, England, Norway and also Scotland." He was undisputed ruler of a North Sea kingdom. He was a natural leader of men.

Like Emperor Charlemagne (d. 814) and many other great leaders, Knut's empire did not survive his death in 1035. Britain went back to native rulers. The end of Scandinavian dominance was at hand. His remains are buried in Winchester Cathedral. He was sort of a "saint" in their eyes.

The Danes had a long established kingdom in the north and east of Britain with Jorvik (York) as its headquarters. Its main political and commercial rival was Dublin, the Norwegian capital of Ireland. Recent archaeological diggings have shown that the ancient Vikings were first class city builders and effective community organizers. The Scandinavian part of Britain was called "Danelaw," the area where Danish laws prevailed. Even today the physical appearance of the people and their language betrays their Nordic past. The big difference between those earlier Vikings and Knut's reign was the civilizing influence of the Christian faith found in Gorm's descendants.

If you go to Denmark, you can visit the site where old King Gorm and his wife, Thyra, are buried. It's near Jelling, a few miles to the northwest of Vejle in Jutland where "Lego" blocks are made. The English still regard Knut, their Danish king, as worthy of London. And the Norwegians also owe a strange debt to Knut. Afterall, it was Knut's ambition for a North Sea empire that propelled Olaf Haraldsson into "sainthood."

However you may feel about Olaf the Saint, this story belongs to Knut. He was also a distant relative of Norway's King Olav V and Denmark's Queen Margaret II. And there are thousands of others who also

claim a share in this royal bloodline but who have no political inheritance. The Danish portion of my household quietly makes such a
claim. Long live Kings Gorm and Knut in the Scandinavian tradition.
And you too, if that's where your heart is.

CHAPTER 32

Thor Heyerdahl—
Discoverer Of "Old Worlds"

FEW PEOPLE HAVE EXCITED THE WORLD with discoveries from past civilizations as Dr. Thor Heyerdahl of Norway. In 1947, he was thrust into international fame by his "Kon-Tiki" voyage. Heyerdahl wanted to test his theory that Polynesia "lay within the range of pre-European mariners from South America."

A thorough going scientist, Heyerdahl was convinced that the people of the Marquesas Islands of the South Pacific were related to the people of pre-Inca Peru. Rejecting popularly held theories that these islands could only have been reached from Asia, he built a balsa raft based on descriptions from early voyages. The wood was cut from the jungles of Ecuador. At the time, the experts said that it would never work. Balsa wood, they claimed, would become water-logged.

The Kon-Tiki sailed from Callao, Peru, on April 28, 1947. 101 days later it ran aground on the coral atoll Raroia in Polynesia, 4300 miles from where it had begun. Heyerdahl never claimed that this proved history had happened in exactly that way but that it "could have happened."

There were days when the weather was too calm and when it was difficult to keep the raft in one piece. Swimming and fishing occupied a good deal of the crew's time. At one point, a 30-foot Whale-Shark followed directly underneath the raft. That was almost as long as the craft itself. At any time it could have upset the raft and plunged the crew of six to their deaths. This interfered with the daily swim and bathing of the sailors.

Fortunately for us, the Kon-Tiki has been preserved in a museum at Bygdoy Park in Oslo. I still remember my excitement when visiting it for the first time. I had read Heyerdahl's book in 1951. To see the preserved raft in near perfect condition was worth the trip overseas for me.

THE SCANDINAVIAN HERITAGE

On a later trip to Norway, I visited with Knut Haugland, a member of the crew and now Director of the Kon-Tiki Museum. Haugland had first achieved fame as a member of the commando team that blew up the heavy water plan at Rjukan in February 1943. He was not at all the burly and tough looking person I had imagined, but rather a quiet mannered gentleman in a business suit who looks like any other Norwegian. I asked him about the Rjukan raid. He answered: "I've put that out of my mind and now like to remember the peacefulness of Polynesia." Later, however, he did discuss the raid with me. Among the things he mentioned was that in 1947 the oceans were clean. Then he showed me some chunks of crude oil found floating on the oceans in recent times and said that there is hardly any place where ocean water is unpolluted today.

Heyerdahl planned several more expeditions. These included the Galapagos Expedition of 1953, the Easter Island Expedition in 1955-1956, the Ra Expeditions of 1969-1970 from Morocco to Barbados and the Tigris Expedition from Iraq to Djibouti in East Africa in 1977-1978. The last one covered 4200 miles while greatly hampered by the troubled political times.

At the conclusion of the Tigris Expedition, the reed boat was ceremonially burned and an appeal was sent to the United Nations on behalf of peace. Heyerdahl is much more than a scientist. He is also a man with a political and social conscience, a trademark of Norwegian foreign policy today.

The Kon-Tiki Museum in Oslo contains many other items besides the raft from that first famous expedition. The pottery collection includes 131 jars of pre-Inca types. There is a model of the Easter Island stone giants and under the Kon-Tiki raft is a replica of the 30-foot whale-shark which bedevilled their journey. It's possible to walk underneath the raft in a life-like setting to see this fearful site through a window.

Heyerdahl is a master of many languages, including English and Polynesian. You would think that English was his native tongue when you read his books. His volume, "The Tigris Expedition," shows him at his best. Aboard was an international crew of 11. They ranged in age from 20 to 63. From the United States came a contractor and a National Geographic cameraman. From the Soviet Union there was a carpenter and a physician who had attended astronauts. There was also crew from Germany, Mexico, Italy, Japan, Denmark, Norway and Iraq.

Heyerdahl now lives in Italy but frequently visits America and Norway. His latest book, "The Maldive Mystery," was published in 1986. I had learned of it in a visit with Knut Haugland, but had no idea of the surprise awaiting me.

CHAPTER 33

The Stave Churches
Of Norway

THERE IS NOTHING SO NORWEGIAN as a stave church, not even lutefisk. Once there were over 1000, today there are only about 30. They can be found as far north as the Folk Museum in Trondheim and as far south as Telemark. These churches were built between the 11th and 14th centuries, almost all before the "Black Death" which struck Norway in 1349.

These timbered structures were built around huge poles planted into the earth and made their appearance about the same time as Christianity entered Norway. The first ones rotted away, but later churches built on sills and beams have survived to this day.

The designs of the stave churches are both ingenious and beautiful. Timbers were selected for size and strength in the days before Norway's forests had been exploited. They are called "stave" churches because of the heavy corner posts and wall planks. When a tree was selected, its branches were trimmed off except for the very top. In this way the tree would die slowly and the lumber would cure. This is why some are still standing after 700-800 years.

The earliest stave church is in the Folk Museum in Oslo's Bygdøy Park. It was moved from Gol in Hallingdal about 100 years ago. Having fallen into disrepair, it is now in excellent condition. The paintings by the altar date from 1652. The "Gol" church has a special interest to me since it was located a few miles from Hemsedal, the home of my earliest family in America who emigrated in 1867.

The largest stave church is called "Heddal" ("Hitterdal") and is located at Notodden in Telemark. It's a huge structure surrounded by a cemetery. It's in excellent condition, having been restored. Both crosses and serpent heads decorate the exterior. The early builders retained some of the images of the pagan past, while committed to the new religion.

It has sometimes been suggested that the architectural design of stave churches resembles the pagodas of Southeast Asia. I asked Kjell Johnsrud of Notodden about this when he showed me the Heddal church. Johnsrud is an authority on lumber and stave church design, being a lumberman himself. He denied any foreign influence and stated that the pattern was authentically Norwegian for its time and the building materials used.

One of the interesting features found in some stave churches is a little window near the altar. It was used to serve communion to people with leprosy. They were not allowed into the churches but were given the sacrament through this opening. Leprosy was a major health problem in western Norway in the Middle Ages due to unsanitary conditions in the homes. In 1873, Dr. G. A. Hansen, a physician from Bergen, isolated the bacillus. Today Norway is free of the disease.

The oldest stave church which remains almost exactly as built is at Borgund in the Sogn region of western Norway. Constructed about 1150, it is one of the best known of these churches and is often seen on pictures. It is the model for the "Chapel in the Hills" near Rapid City, S.D., home of the Lutheran Vespers radio broadcast. Completed in 1969, it's built of fir and cedar and is visited by over 50,000 people each year.

The Hedalen church in Valdres boasts an interesting story of a lost hunter and a bear. During the Black Death, the entire population of some communities was wiped out or people just fled in fear. Years later, a hunter far from home, missed a bird with his arrow and it struck the church bell. After recovering from fright, he investigated and found the lost church and a bear asleep in front of the altar. A bearskin hanging in the church testifies to the tale.

One of the most impressive features of these churches is the wood carvings about the entrances. In some cases, the ceilings are built like the frame of a Viking ship. The origin of these buildings is rooted in mystery, but there is a beauty about them that describes the faith and piety of the people. One tradition tells that St. Olaf made a deal with a troll to build the first one. Whatever it was, they are magnificent structures and remind us of a different Norway than the one we know today.

The stave churches are now a part of Norway's national treasure. If you ever visit this land of the Vikings, don't fail to see at least one of them.

CHAPTER 34

Oslo—"Friendly City Of The North"

THE MOST PICTURESQUE APPROACH to Oslo, Norway's capital city, is by boat. As you travel up the Oslo fjord from Denmark or Germany, the coasts of Norway become visible. The shorelines come closer together and the houses appear in beautiful settings on the mountainsides. Finally, there is Oslo harbor, with the most temperate climate of any capital in northern Europe.

In spite of its far north location, the temperatures in Oslo are pleasant even into October. During the winters, however, sunlight becomes scarce, especially in the valleys. But in the summer, it never gets entirely dark during the days of the "midnight sun." The longest day of the year is celebrated on June 23, St. Hans' Eve or the "Birth of John the Baptist." People light bon fires and many stay up all night to celebrate.

Oslo began as a tiny trading community in 1048. It grew quickly because of its fine harbor. The mountains to the north give it protection from the Arctic winds and the sea to the south brings moderating temperatues from tropical currents. Fire has destroyed the city many times.

In 1624, the Danish ruler, King Christian IV, rebuilt the city close to the Akershus Castle (built about 1300) and renamed it "Christiania," after himself. In 1925, the old name "Oslo" was restored.

When Norway became free of Danish rule in 1814, Sweden's kings became their monarchs until 1905. They agreed, however, to respect Norway's new constitution of May 17, 1814, and to establish Christiania as Norway's capital. So the king had a parliament in both Stockholm and Oslo, but he rarely ever appeared in Norway. Today, one out of every eight people in Norway lives in Oslo, about 500,000 of them. It's recognized as one of the world's most beautiful capitals.

Several things impress me about Norway's chief city. First, it has a vivid sense of history. The name of almost every street has a part of

Norway's "who's who" written into it. Whether it is "Karl Johans Gate" (pronounced "gahtah" and means "street"), "Halvdans Svartes Gate," "Ibsens Gate" or "Gyldenløves Gate," whole volumes could be written about every man after whom a street is named.

Second, the neatness and cleanliness of the city is impressive. There is also the feeling of personal safety as one walks the streets. This is rare in the large cities of the world today. I would suggest, however, obtaining a street map which is available free in most hotels and department stores. It's an old city which grew with no anticipation of 20th century traffic and automobiles. There is excellent public transportation to every part of the metropolitan area.

The third thing which my wife (of Danish ancestry) and I find to be enjoyable about Oslo is the people. They are friendly and polite. Their life styles are different from Americans, not having as much emphasis on night spots and eating out. If you stay in a hotel or guest house, your breakfast ("frokost") will probably be included. These, like the ones we ate at the Continental and Bristol hotels, are such a big spread that there is little need for a noon lunch. However, bakeries and coffee shops offer delicious open-face sandwiches and pastries that delight both eye and stomach.

Everyone who visits Oslo should see Frogner Park and the huge life-like granite statues by Gustav Vigeland. Bygdøy Park which contains the Viking ships, a Folk Museum, the Kon-Tiki Museum and more is worth an afternoon, if not a whole day. Conducted tours are helpful, but they usually don't allow enough time at each of these interesting places. Up on the mountainside to the northwest of the city is Holmenkollen, called the most beautiful ski jump in the world. By the harbor is Akershus, the ancient castle, with the Resistance Museum from World War II. The Oslo Cathedral, "Vor Frelsors Kirke" ("Our Savior's Church"), consecrated in 1897, is a work of art on the inside. A statue of King Christian IV stands on a plaza out in front. Lovers of art will want to visit the National Museum of Art and the Edvard Munch Gallery.

Two buildings dominate the skyline: The City Hall and the Royal Palace. The "Syttende Mai" (17th of May) parade travels from the palace to the "Storting" (parliament building) on Karl Johans Gate alongside of the "Student's Park," site of the old university campus.

Norwegians are proud of their capital city. And if you ever visit it, you'll fall in love with it too.

CHAPTER 35

Akershus—
Fortress Of Old Norway

"NEVER CONQUERED," can be said of very few places in the world. This is the proud boast of "Akershus," a fortress of old Norway. The Oslo harbor is dominated by this castle which was the home of many Norse kings and which has protected their people.

An invasion from Sweden in 1287 prompted the building of this fortification. The walls were built 10 feet thick and over 50 feet high. Building began in 1300 and it was none too soon. There was another invasion from Sweden in 1308 by the king's own son-in-law.

Among the interesting royalty to live in Akershus was Queen Margaret I (1352-1412). It was while living in this castle as an 18-year old queen that she wrote to her husband off in battle: "I want you to know . . . that I as well as my servants suffer from great shortages of food." Then she asked for money "so that those who are with me shall not be separated from me for reason of hunger." The letter was written in late fall. In December, she gave birth to Norway's future king, Olav IV. This castle was no haven of luxury, but it did give protection from its enemies. It was beseiged nine times during the four centuries it served as a fort, but it was never conquered. The last attack was in 1716 by another force from Sweden. The cannons drove off the enemy.

For the next 150 years, the building fell into neglect and disrepair. Forgotten as a part of the nation's defenses, it was used to store equipment and grain. It was not until the 1890s that its historical value was appreciated.

Today, Akershus is an impressive and beautiful landmark. The ancient cannons with their red wooden wheels point out over the harbor like they are ready to challenge any intruder. Cast between 1556 and 1572, they were restored in 1962.

Inside the castle are huge halls and a banquet room, which are used for special state functions. There is also a large memorial in granite on the grounds remembering Norway's dead of World War II. The Resistance Museum of that war is also housed within the walls.

At night, the entire castle area is lit up. To visit this fortress of old Norway gives a person a strong feeling for the country's medieval days. A visitor today gets only the impression of peacefulness on these beautiful grounds. But it has not always been so. Many stormy battles and much bravery have been witnessed here. This is also the place were Vikdun Quisling, the pro-Nazi traitor who urged Hitler to invade Norway, was executed. After a trial which received international press coverage, he faced a firing squad on Oct. 24, 1945, almost six months after his arrest.

Akershus is more than a castle. It is a symbol of the mind and will of Norwegians to be free. If you should go to Norway and have never seen it, make sure that you allow time for it. This medieval castle and Renaissance palace will stay in your memory forever.

CHAPTER 36

Jean Sibelius And
The Music Of Finland

THERE ARE FEW NATIONS whose people I admire so much as Finland. There are few Finns so dearly loved by their countrymen as Jean Sibelius (1865-1957). His portrait of later years depicts a solid executive jaw with drawn cheeks and eyes focused on the future with determination.

Finland has produced many outstanding musicians. Among those who have become well known outside their country are: Erik Tullinberg (1761-1814), the first known Finnish composer; Selim Palmgren (1878-1951), called the Finnish "Chopin;" and Jonas Kokkonen (b. 1921), the leading authority in Finnish music today.

But Sibelius is by common consent the greatest of them all. His "Finlandia" has been playing in my soul since childhood. The hymn, "Thee God, We Praise," is sung to this music, producing an expression of strength and reverence. The music for "Finlandia" was written when Sibelius was in his early 30s. The Russian rulers of Finland sensed its patriotic effect and forbade its performance.

Artists with the ability of Sibelius are not without their eccentric side. To make sure that his studio would have silence while he composed, he built a large "dollhouse" for his five daughters at a safe distance from his residence. This is in contrast to Edvard Grieg who built a "composing cottage" at a distance from his house in Bergen. Still he was warm-hearted to his family and townsmen. Guests were served wines of rare vintage. As a young man, he fell in love with Vienna and the waltzes of Strauss.

Sibelius imitated no other musicians. His work flowed out of the loneliness and lofty aspirations of his own soul. The violin was his first love. He would stand in the bow of a boat and play to the birds and waves, reproducing the sounds of the wind, clouds and rustling branches. The Finnish epic myths, "Kalevala," influenced his musical expressions of patriotism. A magnificent concert hall has been erected in

103

Helsinki in honor of Sibelius where over 200 concerts a year are held.

Finland passed from Swedish to Russian rule in 1809. Not until Dec. 6, 1917, did Finland gain independence. During the Winter War of 1939-1940, Sibelius, then 74, refused to go into an air-raid shelter. Instead, he angrily charged out into the cold with an old hunting rifle and fired away at the Russian bombers.

Finns are a proud and patriotic people. It's true that they are often criticized for being careful not to publicly offend the Kremlin. But no nation has been so conscientious about repaying its war debts to the United States. In the secret conferences of World War II between the Allied leaders, Churchill and Roosevelt refused to allow Stalin to reclaim Finland as Russian territory.

Music continues to inspire love for native land in the hearts of the Finns. Over 60 music institutes perpetuate this heritage in this land of nearly 5,000,000 people, 70,000 lakes and 200,000 reindeer. This little nation boasts 11 symphony orchestras. Over 60,000 people attend the annual folk music festival in Kaustinen, a city of only 3400. The world needs more people like the Finns. So if you are Finnish, you have reason to be proud.

CHAPTER 37

Sweden—
Its People And Royalty

SWEDEN IS THE LARGEST of the Scandinavian countries. Almost 8,500,000 people live in 173,630 square miles, a little larger than California. This northern country is warmed by the Gulf Stream in the Atlantic and is surprisingly mild. Sweden has almost 100,000 lakes and over half of it is covered with forests. Over 2,500,000 people live in three cities: Stockholm, Goteborg and Malmo. And they still eat lutefisk for Christmas.

A glacier covered northern Europe 15,000 years ago. About 9000 years ago, fishermen and hunters began to settle in Sweden. Then about 2500 years ago, another Ice Age began which lasted 400 years. The present inhabitants of Sweden, as well as Denmark and Norway, are a part of the Teutonic migration that came from Germany.

The center of power in early Sweden was the "Svea" tribe near Uppsala. The name "Sweden" is derived from them. Many historians also identify the "Goths" who spread over Europe to have originally migrated from Sweden.

Once the center of Viking activity, Swedish traders and soldiers of fortune travelled eastward into Russia and then southward to Constantinople. They established the first kingdom of Russia at Kiev and many became known as "Varangians," the Greek emperor's elite palace guard. The name "Rus," modern "Russia," originally meant Sweden.

In those Viking days, the worship of Odin, Thor and Frey struck terror in the hearts of the people with their great appetite for human sacrifice. It was the Christian missionaries from Germany and England who gave them new directions.

In 1397, Sweden was joined to Denmark and Norway in the Union of Kalmar. In 1523, the Vasa family came to power and created an independent Sweden. They also established the Lutheran Reformation. The most famous of these Vasa kings was Gustav II Adolf (Gustavus

Adolphus), known as the "Lion of the North." Swedish immigrants founded a college at St. Peter, Minnesota, after his name in 1862.

The Vasa family ran out of heirs in the early 1800s and made an agreement with Napoleon to invite his Marshall, Jean Baptiste Jules Bernadotte, to become the crown prince. He accepted and took the name "Karl Johan." Then he switched sides over to the British for which he was rewarded by being given Norway. He was not Norway's choice of king, but did prove to be a good ruler for them.

The Bernadottes continue as the royal family of Sweden and are very popular both in Sweden and among Swedes in America. The present king, Carl XVI Gustaf, was given solid academic preparation for his ceremonial position. His wife, Sylvia, is of German and Brazilian background. Crown Prince Harald of Norway is also a Bernadotte through his mother, the late Crown Princess Martha.

Sweden has had peace since 1814 and this contributes towards its great progress in science, statesmanship, and for its leadership in Christian humanitarianism. This is also why so many of Sweden's magnificent architecture of the past remains for us to see when we visit Stockholm. In 1976, Sweden elected a non-socialist Prime Minister and continues its cautious neutralist policies. In a world of so much conflict, there is much we can learn from the Swedes.

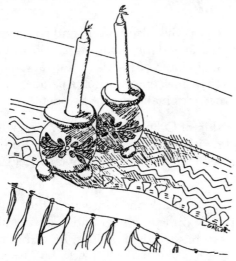

Swedish candlesticks.

CHAPTER 38

H. C. Andersen—
Denmark's Beloved Storyteller

I N NEW YORK CITY'S CENTRAL PARK, there is a statue of Denmark's favorite storyteller. Around it gather crowds of children to hear his fairy tales. Many suppose him to be American, but Hans Christian Andersen is still the pride of Denmark. Next to the Bible, his writings are the most widely read and translated in the world. Who is this Dane that so many people have come to love?

Hans was born April 2, 1805, at Odense on the island of Fyn, the son of a shoemaker and a washerwoman. His father died when he was only nine and his mother 20 years later. How did this boy, reared in poverty and obscurity, rise to become so famous that when he died on Aug. 4, 1875, his funeral was held in the Copenhagen Cathedral? Nearest the coffin sat the royal family, foreign ambassadors and other impressive guests.

Great writers have a streak of loneliness in their souls. Despite his fame and his welcome into the homes of the most famous people of Europe, he never owned a house nor did he marry. There were loves in his life, but it was usually fantasy. His self-centeredness and his strange appearance got in the way. He was his own "ugly duckling." Even his most friendly critics noted that he wrote mostly about himself.

Despite his loneliness and outsider role, Andersen was a great entertainer and reporter of his times. He had a love-hate relationship with royalty. At the time, kings were held to be above criticism, except in France where Louis XVI was beheaded. He enjoyed royal favor, but in his writing he showed contempt for the vanity of blue-bloods. In private papers found after his death, he wrote: "I maintain that the Shoemaker's Guild is the most famous, for I am the son of a shoemaker."

Andersen was a deeply religious man, despite his father's atheism. He did not, however, accept conventional creeds. When questioned about his beliefs, he claimed: "I have become convinced that what Christ teaches in fact comes from God." He was at odds over theology with two other famous Danes, Bishop Grundtvig and Soren Kierkegaard.

Andersen was a legend in his own time and was the most photographed person of his day. He was one of the most widely travelled Danes, but never visited America. He wrote: "What a pity that America lies so far away from here." He was a pen-pal of Longfellow in Massachusetts and visited Dickens in England. He made 29 journeys abroad and wrote 156 fairy tales and stories.

Some of his works include "The Emperor's New Clothes" and "Red Shoes," as well as "The Ugly Duckling." My favorite Andersen fairy tale is "The Snow Queen." It's the story of a little girl named Gerda who rescues her friend Kaj from the ice castle of the wicked Snow Queen.

If we could rescue the world's political and military leaders from their fears for a week and gather them to read Andersen's fairy tales, there just might be a chance for peace in our times.

Home of Hans Christian Andersen.

CHAPTER 39

How Scandinavia Became Christian

THE STRUGGLE BETWEEN GOOD AND EVIL in our world has many surprises. Who would have guessed that the descendants of the ancient Vikings, once the terror of the Christian world, would become the sponsors of the "Peace Prize" in our time?

A great deal of mystery surrounds the beginnings of those fury-filled bandits of the North Sea lands. On Easter Sunday, 617, they descended on the Island of Eigg off the coast of Scotland and massacred the 54 monks who lived there. For the next 400 years, no one would live in safety from their raids. The greatest outrage came on June 8, 793, when they sacked the holy island of Lindisfarne, off the northeast coast of England. Shockwaves were felt in the courts of Emperor Charlemagne in France.

The first missionary of distinction to make inroads into these lands was St. Ansgar who had come from France. He made significant beginnings as the missionary Archbishop of Bremen before he died in 865.

England set the stage for the Christian assault on the Viking lands. Much credit has to go to one of its most famous kings, Alfred the Great, for saving his land from the onslaught of the pagan Danes. Combining Christian learning and brilliant military skills, he defeated the Danes and then peacefully persuaded their general, Guthrum, to be baptized in 878. Alfred stood as godfather at the ceremony. From England, the new faith spread back to Denmark. It took a while, but in 965 King Harald "Bluetooth" declared Denmark to be a Christian nation. A stone marked with runic carvings testifies to his words at Jelling in Jutland. My wife and I made a special stop to see it.

It was the story of the "strong Christ" rather than the "gentle Jesus" that converted the Northmen. The Vikings were not a happy people, as we might have supposed. Harsh climate, scarcity of food and the tyranny of pagan gods filled their lives with fear. The Christ whose voice

109

commanded the sea waves and who healed the lepers gave them a new hope. The brutality in their plundering stemmed from the pent up rage which they felt against these forces. "Pity," for the first time, entered their society.

Norway was more obstinate to the missionaries than Denmark. It was the relentless striving of the English bishops that moved two kings named Haakon and two kings named Olaf back to Norway on missionary crusades. The claims of Bishop Grimkel, who promoted the "St. Olaf" legend, completed the turn of events which won the day for the "White Christ."

King Olaf Erickson of Sweden, influenced by a martyred monk from Glastonbury, led Sweden into Christian ways. Finland was reached through Bishop Henry, also English, who had spent time in Sweden. He was martyred on Jan. 19, 1156. Iceland's decision to be Christian was made by a pagan Law-Giver, who decided it would be best for the land. He might have been "influenced" by the fear of Norway's King Olaf Tryggvason.

It touched my heart deeply to see the headquarters of the Nobel Peace Prize in Oslo, knowing that in Norway more blood was shed for the conversion of a nation than anywhere else in Scandinavia. I still believe in miracles.

A statue from Gausdal Church, Oppland.

CHAPTER 40

Oscar Overby—
"He Taught Us To Sing"

THERE ARE A FEW PEOPLE, maybe not many, that we wish would live forever. Oscar R. Overby (1892-1964) is one of those people on my list. He first came to my attention through the music he wrote for church choirs. These were also commonly used by high school and college choral groups.

My first look at Overby came at a Luther League Convention at Milwaukee in 1947. In those days of the former Evangelical Lutheran Church (ELC), every gathering involved a "Choral Union." In Milwaukee, Overby directed 2000 singers. His technique and charm made it fun to sing. It wasn't until 1953 that I came to know him personally. As the Executive Director of the ELC's Choral Union, he came to Bottineau, N.D., to hold a Church Music Institute. He had us sing hymns, both old and new, and made them exciting and unforgettable. I remember singing them in my mind for weeks afterwards.

Who was this unusually gifted and humble man? He was born Sept. 25, 1892, on a farm along the Sheyenne River 10 miles northeast of Cooperstown, N.D. His parents had come from Ostmaerka in eastern Norway in 1882. The Norwegian language was so much a part of their culture that they even played baseball in the mother tongue during recess at school. A teacher offered 50 cents to any pupil who could stay away from Norwegian for a week. No one collected.

Overby completed his high school at Concordia Academy (now College) in Moorhead, MN, in 1912. He went on to St. Olaf College in Northfield, MN, and to the New England Conservatory of Music in Boston. World War I called him into military service.

In 1921, Overby joined the music faculty at St. Olaf where he remained until 1948. There he worked with the famed F. Melius Christiansen. His wife, Gertrude Boe Overby (1900-1979), was from Finley, N.D. She was a famous soloist in her day and continued to sing with the St. Olaf Choir for many years after graduation.

THE SCANDINAVIAN HERITAGE

In the private memoirs written for his family, Overby mentioned a few former students of whom he was especially proud. Among these are Paul J. Christiansen of Concordia College in Moorhead, Minn., John Strohm of Minot State College in North Dakota (now both retired), and Frank Pooler of Long Beach State College in California. I have never met a former student of his who didn't have the highest respect and affection for him.

In 1948, Overby became the Executive Director of the ELC's Choral Union. His memoirs note two trips to Minot, N.D., in 1954 and 1955. At one of these "a Danish Catholic Priest directed his boy's choir which sang 'Den store hvide flok' in good Norwegian."

Forty-eight hundred singers sang together for Overby in Minneapolis for the Lutheran World Federation Assembly in 1957. He called this "the super-climax of all my experiences in directing massed chorus singing."

Prof. Strohm said of Overby: "He had that unique quality of being able to communicate with everybody." Overby's own definition of music was: "Music is Christian love in search of a word." Many of us owe a great debt to Oscar Overby. He taught us to sing.

CHAPTER 41

The "Resistance Museum" In Oslo

THE SIGN AT THE ENTRANCE to Norway's Resistance Museum reads: "NEVER AGAIN." The Museum is located at Akershus Castle in Oslo's harbor. It was opened on May 8, 1970, by Crown Prince Harald, exactly 25 years after peace and constitutional government was restored. The purpose of the Museum is for "the young people of today and the coming generations."

It is still an embarrassment for Norway that it was so ill prepared to defend itself in 1940. But it's easy to understand. Norway had not been in a military conflict since 1814. The people trusted in their neutrality. None of its military leaders had been in a war. But 61 bitter months of occupation convinced its leaders that "never again" shall this happen. Despite its uneasiness about sharing a border with the Soviet Union, Norway is a cooperative member of NATO.

It was an unforgettable experience for my wife and myself to have been through the Museum, personally escorted by the Director, Reidar Thorpe. He had been a part of the Resistance. We learned that the last person he took through the Museum had been the US Secretary of Navy. He told us that the most important part of the Resistance was to help Norwegians to stand up against the Nazi propaganda to collaborate with the enemy. The Gestapo used both promises and cruelty to bend people's wills.

The name "Quisling" has come down in history as a term of shame. He was the leader of a small political party called "National Unity." It was Vikdun Quisling that urged Hitler to "save" Norway from the British and the Communists. Before the war, Quisling collected less than 2000 votes. At the end of the war, 40,000 had joined him, most of them quite innocently unaware of his Hitler connections. The underground newspapers led the cause for truth to the people. Dignity, calmness and discipline were the watchwords of Resistance leaders.

The Museum, called "Norges Hjemmefrontmuseum," is well researched and designed. Maps, secret papers, photos and audio-visuals bring the war years vividly to the visitor's awareness in 48 displays.

The saddest part was to see the torture tools used by the Gestapo. At the Grini Prison Camp near Oslo, 19,000 Norwegians were detained. 9000 more were sent to Germany, of whom 1340 died, including 610 Jewish Norwegians.

Germany and Norway have traditionally been friends, having bonds through church, commerce and culture. The well kept German cemeteries in Norway are a testimony to this. I visited one in Trondheim. It was heart rending to see the grave markers of so many youth who died for the follies of evil rulers.

A sign of the Resistance Movement was to wear a paper clip in a coat lapel. It means: "Let's Keep Together."

If you ever visit Oslo, be sure to visit the Resistance Museum. You will never forget it. Americans need to be reminded too that the price of freedom is "eternal vigilance." We all need to do our part so that this will "never again" happen in the lands we love.

CHAPTER 42

Ole Rolvaag—
A "Giant In The Earth"

HE WAS ONLY 55 WHEN HE DIED IN 1931. But the boy from the island of Donna near the Arctic Circle had become world famous. Ole Edvart Rolvaag was born April 22, 1876. Six generations of the family had lived on this rocky, wind-swept and treeless cove.

Fishing was the main business of the community, but Ole's father was also a good carpenter and did some small farming. They grew barley, rye, potatoes and raised a few cattle and sheep. The chief interest of the Rolvaag family, however, was literary. By age six, everyone was expected to start reading. This did not come easy for Ole. Formal education began at age seven. There were three terms of three weeks each during the year. The only road to the schoolhouse seven miles away was a rough path. School ended with Confirmation at age 14. Then he was off to apprentice with a fishing captain.

Fortunately, Ole did learn how to read well, but it was the storytelling during the long winter nights that stirred his imagination. When he read "The Last of the Mohicans," a story about life in the New World, a new idea began to take root in his mind. After a terrible sea storm off the Lofoten Islands, where many sailors were drowned, Ole resolved to go to America. An uncle at Elk Point, S.D., sent him a ticket. His employer offered to buy him a sleek new fishing boat if he would forget about America. Ole stuck to his plans.

After working on his uncle's farm in South Dakota, Ole decided that milking cows and cleaning barns was not the job for him. Afterall, that was women's work in Norway. A pastor encouraged him to get an education. At age 23, Ole entered Augustana Acdademy at Canton, S.D. He graduated in two years with honors. There he met Jennie Marie Berdahl, the daughter of a pioneer family, who later became his wife. It was from her relatives that he received much of the information about pioneer life. In the fall of 1901, Ole began his studies at St. Olaf College. He did so well that Pres. Kildahl wanted him to become a pastor.

But Ole decided he would be a teacher and a position was offered him at St. Olaf where he remained for the rest of his life. During the summer of 1904, he taught parochial school at Bisbee and Churches Ferry, N.D.

At St. Olaf, Rolvaag had a double career as a professor and a writer. He was always a close friend of students in need. It was during these years that he wrote his most famous book, "Giants In The Earth." His tragic hero, Per Hansa, is immortal to all who have read this novel. It was a Book of the Month Club selection in 1927. "Peder Victorious" and "Their Father's God" completed the trilogy.

Though he was of only modest stature and suffering from heart problems in later life, it was pride and will power that propelled the boy from the windswept island of the North to become a "giant." On the St. Olaf campus, the library memorializes this professor who has given us the most vivid description of immigrant life among the Norwegians on the Dakota prairies.

Many people called "giants" are misfits in society. Rolvaag, however, was known by his friends as one who loved life. He has added much to our appreciation for living.

CHAPTER 43

T. F. Gullixson—
As I Remember Him

I FIRST HEARD HIS ELOQUENT VOICE in the Spring of 1944. His theme, "We Live To Bequeath," still rings in my memory. The words were a manifesto of the life he lived. Thaddaeus Francke Gullixson was born Sept. 4, 1882, on a homestead in the Des Moines River Valley near Bode, Iowa.

His early days on the farm taught him the love of land and the sacredness of community. It also imbedded in his soul the value of hard work and the awareness of human frailty. In one of his books, he tells the story of driving a team of runaway horses pulling an empty hayrack and how his father's strong arms and voice brought the team to a halt. In the years to come, he saw his father's hands as the hands of God.

"Tad," as they called him, was needed on the farm as older brother, George, was ordained into the ministry when Tad was only 11. But Tad was to follow. He attended Bruflat Academy in Portland, N.D., and then went on to Luther College in Decorah, Iowa. After completing theological studies at Luther Seminary in St. Paul, Minnesota, he spent the academic year 1906-1907 at Johns Hopkins University in Baltimore. It promised to be a brilliant career in Old Testament studies. He mentioned his graduate studies to me on a couple of occasions. Each time a "light" came into his aging eyes. But then came a Letter of Call from a "West River" congregation in Pierre, S.D.

In 1911, after four years of ministering to cowboys on the frontier, he became the pastor of First Lutheran Church in Minot, N.D., where he remained until 1930. His mark on the community is still keenly felt by the many who knew him. His concern for the community has been memorialized by Trinity Medical Center of which he was a founder and board chairman. One of his cherished friends in Minot was Ragnvald Nestos, who was governor of North Dakota from 1921-1925.

For 25 years, from 1930-1955, Gullixson was president of Luther Theological Seminary in St. Paul and at the same time was vice-president of the former Norwegian Lutheran Church in America, later named Evangelical Lutheran Church. My closest contact with "Dr. Gullixson," as we students always called him, was from 1948-1954. When I graduated from seminary in 1952, it was his encouragement that brought me back to the campus to earn an advanced degree in 1956.

His personal life and views were never the primary subject of his lectures, conversations or sermons. But these things did drop here and there and they were gathered as precious gems by those of us who were in his presence. O. G. Malmin, former editor of the "Lutheran Herald," described Gullixson's preaching as "biblical, confessional and contemporary." I would add the word "doxological" or the "praise of God" to this list.

Gullixson had a keen musical ability. While pastor in Minot, he was also choir director. He was on the editorial board of the popular hymnal called the "Concordia." He was also a member of the Joint Union Committee which guided the formation of the American Lutheran Church in 1960.

The eminent seminary president was like a "father" to many of us who received our professional education under his influence. While he could be uncompromising in the presence of his peers, he never forgot what it was like to be a boy. Toughness and gentleness were close together in his spirit. In the fall of 1949, he spoke in chapel for a week on the theme "No Minimums" in scholarship, humility, faithfulness, courage and patience. His words had a way of taking deep root in the listener's soul. I can still hear that voice with its majestic cadence and vibrato. We considered ourselves fortunate if he would ever invite us into his office just to chat. We valued every moment of it.

When he died on April 2, 1969, an era ended for many of us. Just five days later on April 7, Easter Monday, another era ended for me. My own father died. I had lost two "fathers" in one week. "We live to bequeath" was a fitting epitaph for both of them.

CHAPTER 44

Rjukan—Norway's Heavy Water Plant Attacked

THE DRIVE WEST FROM OSLO through Drammen, Kongsberg and Notodden is a delight to the eyes. As the mountains grow more beautiful, the terrain becomes more rugged. Thirty-five miles north is Rjukan ("Rookaan"), one of the most important Allied targets during World War II.

On the evening of Feb. 27, 1943, nine Norwegians, led by Knut Haukelid and trained in Great Britain by the SOE ("Special Operations Executive"), climbed down a steep and icy mountainside, crossed a river and climbed up another mountain to a heavily guarded factory which produced "heavy water." They eluded the guards, broke into the factory, poured out the water and planted explosives. They fled unseen. A massive search by 3000 soldiers could not find them.

What was it all about? "Heavy water" or "deuterium oxide" looks and tastes like other water, but it isn't. It was produced at the Norsk Hydro plant under Nazi supervision for building atomic bombs for Hitler. Rjukan was his only source of this rare liquid.

In 1939, Albert Einstein wrote to President Roosevelt that such a weapon was possible. In June 1942, Churchill visited FDR. Rjukan was heavy on his mind. He knew the danger if Hitler should get such a weapon.

Four months later, a bomber took off from Scotland with highly trained Norwegian saboteurs. The Hardanger Plateau below was an unfriendly place to drop by parachute. One of these young men was Knut Haugland, an expert wireless operator. To see this peaceful looking man today, you would never guess that he had been on that death defying mission.

Rjukan is located in a valley only 300 yards wide. The defenses seemed impregnable. However, a patriotic Norwegian scientist was in charge of the plant. It was fortunate too that Prof. Leif Tronstad of Trondheim had fled to England. He had designed the factory and was

119

able to build a mock-up of it so that the saboteurs knew their way around in it even if blindfolded. Microphotographs were smuggled in toothpaste tubes into Sweden and then to London.

The nine men who made the journey had suffered intensely for months on the cold, barren and windy plateau. Their food supplies had not lasted long enough. Reinforcements towed in gliders had perished. When they killed a reindeer, they ate "the whole thing."

By fall, the plant had been rebuilt and Hitler's timetable was back on schedule. A British air raid did little damage but killed 21 Norwegians. In February 1944, a large shipment of heavy water was ready to send to Germany. A ferry boat was to carry it over Lake Tinnsjo and out to sea. Saboteurs, led by Haukelid and dressed as workmen, planted explosives on board. At the deep end of the lake, an explosion rocked the belly of the ship. In four minutes it was gone. Hitler did not get his bomb.

The mountains around Rjukan are quiet today. But the valleys are alive with the memories of those days. If you ever visit Oslo, take a trip to Rjukan and see it for yourself. It's a part of the Scandinavian heritage.

CHAPTER 45

Viking
Burial Customs

T HE BEST KNOWN OF THE VIKING SHIPS is the "Gokstad," built about 850 A.D. The Minnesota built "Hjemkomst" is modelled after it. When I first saw the Gokstad ship in the museum at Bygdøy Park in Oslo, one thing fascinated me most. Just behind the middle is a "burial chamber." It seems so strange that this beautiful ship had been hauled ashore and buried in the blue clay as a part of a royal funeral. Buried with the king were 12 horses, six dogs and a peacock. Except for this custom, we would never have known this famous vessel. Why did the burial take place in this manner? It was so the king could go to Paradise in style.

Not everyone, of course, can be buried in a "Cadillac." But there are some interesting things found in the Viking cemeteries. Three principal burial grounds that have been studied are Birka in Sweden, Hedeby in south Slesvig (now Germany) and Lindholm Hoje near Aalborg in northern Jutland (Denmark).

Both burials and cremations took place. For the rich, there were large burial chambers, usually reserved for men. Sometimes a favorite wife and a slave were also buried. Women were usually placed in more modest wooden coffins. The old Viking religion looked upon death as a journey for which a person needed food, weapons, animals and companions.

When Christianity came, cremations were forbidden. It was held to be a denial of the Christian doctrine of the resurrection. The teaching of resurrection is quite different from the various views on the "immortality of the soul," which prefer quick disposal of the body. Christians placed their coffins in an east-west position as a sign of their faith.

When boats were too expensive, Vikings placed rocks around the grave in the shape of a boat. Once a person was safely dead, the rocks could be removed and used for another grave. If a person's ghost gave trouble to the family, they would reopen the grave and calm the spirit with a spear.

Large mounds often mark burial sites. Such is the case at Jelling in southern Jutland. Here King Harald "Bluetooth" buried his pagan father, King Gorm, and his mother, Queen Thyri. Two large mounds marked by runestones identify the site. On one of these markers, Harald is memorialized, "He made the Danes Christians." My wife and I have stood on top of the mounds.

Viking graves have also been found in Russia, Scotland, England, Ireland, the North Sea Islands, Holland, Normandy and Poland. In Russia, the Swedes ("Rus") preferred cremation. The Arab ambassador at Kiev was told: "You Arabs are foolish. You throw those you love and honor to the ground where the earth and the maggots and fields devour them, whereas we, on the other hand, burn them up quickly and they go to Paradise that very moment."

Burial customs reflected the views of "afterlife." The Viking beliefs were often fuzzy. This is one reason given why Christianity triumphed in those lands. The next time you see a Viking ship or even a picture of one, remember that they were used for more than sailing. It was the way to buried in style for those who could afford it.

CHAPTER 46

Soren Kierkegaard—
A Dane Whose Ideas Outlived Him

D ANES ARE SUPPOSED TO BE of two varieties, happy ones and gloomy ones. That is, of course, an oversimplification. I know many who are serious about life and yet delightful company. Soren Kierkegaard (1813-1855) was called the "melancholy Dane." He has left a permanent mark on the world for being the "father of existentionalism," a philosophy that struggles to find meaning to life.

Soren's father was a dominating influence in the home. As a little boy, he had lived in western Jutland, the same area from which my wife's family (Kirkegaard) originates. He had herded sheep alone in the open land, summer and winter, in all kinds of weather. This can be lonely. One day, he became so depressed that he stood on a sand dune and cursed God for his unhappy existence.

When Soren's father was 12, he moved with his family to Copenhagen. He grew up to become a wealthy merchant. At age 40, haunted by his past, he transferred his business to a relative and devoted all his time to his family. He must have been a hardy man as he lived to be 82. Soren was born when his father was 56.

Like his father, Soren had a brilliant mind and a melancholy spirit. He anguished over the meaning of life. He also inherited a vivid imagination. His father would take his hand and they would walk around the table imagining that they were in a forest or going past a bakery on a crowded street, with all the noises and smells of the city.

A stern brand of Christianity was taught in the Kierkegaard home. Sin and holiness were seen as "black and white," with no shades of gray. When he entered the University, Soren rebelled against the religion of his home. This caused a break with his father, though they were later reconciled.

At age 28, a traumatic event occurred in Soren's life. He was engaged to marry Regine Olsen. But he brooded over his unworthiness of her so much that he broke the engagement, despite Regine's contrary feelings. His condition has been described as "manic-depressive psychosis." He went from highest exultation to deepest depression. From the writings of Martin Luther, he learned how to face his suffering.

He had a running battle with the State Church. Though he graduated from seminary, he was never ordained. His attack was not on the Christian faith but against "rationalism" in the church, which made reason rather than Scripture the authority for faith. God was always a serious encounter for him. He saw truth as "dialectic," that is, in opposite pairs. If God was holy, then Soren was sinful. His method of thinking has influenced both Christian and atheistic existentionalism. He was a prolific writer. Among his best known books are "Fear and Trembling," "Either/Or," and "Edifying Discourses."

While I do not claim to be a "Kierkegaardian" (except by marriage), there is much of value that I have learned from this famous Danish religious thinker. He remains one of Denmark's greatest influences on the world. He was a Dane whose ideas outlived him.

CHAPTER **47**

The Scandinavians
In North Dakota

SCANDINAVIANS SEEM TO BE everywhere in North Dakota. While this is the most Scandinavian state in the U.S., there are a few places where they forgot to come. But they are all here: Danes, Finns, Icelanders, Norwegians and Swedes.

A helpful book to locate the Scandinavians in the state has been written by William C. Sherman, entitled "Prairie Mosaic: An Ethnic Atlas of North Dakota." He writes of the Norwegians: "A venturesome soul could walk (with an occasional detour) from the Garrison Dam to the northwest corner of the state without stepping off Norwegian-owned land." He has platted every township in the state for its ethnic heritage. Another book of interest is "Ethnic Heritage in North Dakota," edited by Francie M. Berg. Those looking for information on Scandinavians in it will be delighted.

The major settlement of Danes is north of Kenmare, mainly in Renville County. They began to arrive in 1889. A Danish windmill beckons tourists to the community. Danes settled in eight of North Dakota's 53 counties.

The largest community of Finns is in Rolla in Rolette County and Rock Lake in Towner County. The earliest settlers came in 1896. Nine counties became home for Finns in the state.

The Icelanders first settled around Mountain in Pembina County. They had originally settled in Manitoba in 1875 and relocated to North Dakota in 1878. In 1886, a migration of 30 families began a relocation to Upham in McHenry County. These are the only two Icelandic areas in the state.

There are numerous Swedish communities in 21 counties. The most concentrated area is found west of Washburn in McLean County and over into Burleigh County. The Fargo, Grand Forks and Minot areas attracted quite a number of Swedish immigrants who still live there.

125

THE SCANDINAVIAN HERITAGE

Norwegians have settlements in 42 counties, with major groups in 25 counties. They began arriving about 1870 in Trail County along the eastern edge of the state. The Red River Valley was "flooded" with immigrants from all parts of Norway. The Goose and Sheyenne rivers attracted many of them. Fargo, Grand Forks, Valley City, Devils Lake, Minot and Williston are major centers of Norwegian-American population.

From the beginning, the Scandinavians were fanatic about educating their children. As a result, large numbers of them became leaders in business, politics, education and social services in the state. Many have also left North Dakota for employment elsewhere.

Love for heritage is expressed by Scandinavians through the annual Norsk Høstfest celebration each October in Minot. Over 20,000 people attended in 1983 to greet Princess Astrid of Norway, including many from Scandinavia. Attendance grew to 35,000 in 1986.

As a boy growing up in a Norwegian home in Richland County, I discovered Germans while attending a rural grade school. Imagine my surprise, when I learned that Martin Luther was German too! I dearly love those lands across the sea, but I am grateful to my forebearers who arranged for me to grow up in the opportunities of the New World.

CHAPTER 48

"Munkholmen" In The Trondheim Harbor

STANDING HIGH ON A PILLAR in the center of Trondheim's business district is a statue of King Olaf Tryggvason. He founded the city about A.D. 996 when the assembly ("Thing") chose him to be king over all Norway. Out in the harbor, under Olaf's watchful eye, is a little island which has been witness to much of Norway's history.

The island is called "Munkholmen." When Olaf clashed with the pagan Norwegians in the area, he hung the head of their leader, Earl Haakon, on the gallows as a warning to all the people on shore that they should not resist his new Christian rule. At that time, Munkholmen was used as a place of executions. His statue has Earl Haakon's head by his feet.

In 1105, Benedictine monks built a monastery on the island. That is why it's called "Munkholmen" ("Monk Island") to this day. It was one of 35 monasteries built in Norway. Monasteries and cathedrals became centers of wealth in those days, accumulating large tracts of land for farming. It remained a home for monks until 1531, when the Reformation came to Norway.

In later years, the Danish government used the island as a military fortress and as a prison for enemies of the king. One such prisoner was Peter Schumacher, a brilliant young man of German background who rose to great power in the kingdom. He was known as "Count Griffenfeld." Power, however, went to his head. He was loyal to King Christian V (1670-1699), but the nobles were jealous of him. Because he opposed a war with Sweden, he was branded a traitor and brought to the place of execution. The gallows were ready and the axe was raised. Then came the king's reprieve and he was sent to prison, first in Copenhagen for four years and then to Munkholmen for 18 years.

I listened to the guide tell Griffenfeld's story. At first, he had been allowed to read and write. When pen and ink were taken away, he tore bits of lead from the windows and wrote comments on the margins of books. It must have been a cold, damp and lonely place. His health totally broken, he was released in 1698, but died the following year at age 64.

During World War II, the Nazis mounted anti-aircraft guns on top of the ancient castle. It gave me an eerie feeling to stand where Nazi gunners had stood and to realize that they controlled the shoreline all the way from the northern tip of Norway to Africa during my high school days.

Today, Munkholmen looks like the most peaceful place in the world. It's a tourist attraction where you can buy a lunch and stroll around in perfect ease. You can walk the steps of the castle from its dungeon up to the turret. If you ever visit Trondheim, get on a ferry boat and visit Munkholmen. Then let your imagination enjoy itself. You may see King Olaf Tryggvason, the Benedictine monks, Count Griffenfeld and even the Nazis. And if you ever make such a trip, I hope it will be a sunny day for you like it was for our family. It's a place and a story that you will never forget.

CHAPTER 49

Hans Nielsen Hauge—
Norway's Greatest Folk Hero

NOBODY HAS HAD SO GREAT an influence on the people of Norway in modern times as Hans Nielsen Hauge. This influence was carried to the New World by over 800,000 immigrants.

Who was Hauge and why was he so important? He was born on April 3, 1771, about 50 miles southeast of Oslo. The "Hauge Gaard" (farm) was small and could afford Hans only a minimal education. Yet he learned the three "R's" well and was good at carpentry and blacksmithing. He even invented his own tools and he had a good head for business.

Despite these practical skills, his foremost interest was religion. Hans was reared in a pious home with daily Bible reading, prayers and where the catechism was studied together with Luther's sermons. Hans went with his parents to Bible studies led by laymen. One question bothered him: "What does God require of me?" So he applied himself to studying Scripture and theology at home. Though everything was clear in his head, his heart was full of uncertainty. One day when he was 25, while singing a hymn behind a plow, he felt he was being lifted to heaven. This changed his life and Hans was persuaded that God had called him to be a "preacher."

Hauge travelled over 10,000 miles to almost every part of Norway in all kinds of weather. The common people responded to him with enthusiasm. But there was a law which forbade unauthorized persons from preaching. The authorities were afraid that he might lead a peasant revolt. Between 1796 and 1804, he was arrested 10 times and accused of all kinds of crimes, including murder and witchcraft.

The authorities in Copenhagen decided that Hauge would have to be punished. He was taken to Akershus Castle and locked in a soggy dungeon for several years. Later he was put into a small room with a barred window in a two-story house for 10 years. Today, visitors can see this house in Bygdøy Park, chains and all.

Hauge had proven business skills and had built paper mills, grist mills, printing houses and salt factories. These supported his evangelistic work which was carried out through many friends. During a war with England in 1809, he was released from jail to build more salt factories, as Norway's supplies were cut off.

Though opposed by the State Church, Hauge held no bitterness. One of his sons became a pastor in the State Church in Skien. His health broke under the strain of prison and he was released at Christmas 1814 upon paying a heavy fine. Since he could travel no more, a constant stream of visitors came to him until he died 10 years later.

Today, Hauge is honored throughout Norway and especially in the churches where he was once forbidden to speak. In America, there was a "Hauge Synod" among Norwegian Lutherans. Though he emphasized repentance and personal faith, yet he also is recognized in Norway today as a "folk leader" among the common people. He could never forget that he was the son of a farmer. I know the feeling.

CHAPTER 50

Grundtvig—The Most Danish Of The Danes

I T WAS THE SUMMER OF 1954 when the Ox Creek Church near Rolette, N.D., celebrated its 65th anniversary. Since it had been founded by Norse settlers, a Norwegian service was planned. One hymn was the unanimous choice of the old timers: "Kirken den er et gammelt hus" ("Built on a rock the Church shall stand"). Translated literally, it means "The church is an old house." It was written by one of Denmark's most famous sons, Nikolai Frederik Severin Grundtvig. He was born Sept. 8, 1783, the youngest of five to a parsonage family on Zeeland (Sjaeland), Denmark's largest island.

Nikolai was taught by his mother to love literature, history, poetry and Norse mythology. At age nine, he left home for boarding schools and did not return to live with his parents until after he had graduated from the University in Copenhagen.

Though he had graduated from seminary, he was not ordained until he was 38. His father became ill and needed help. On his first Sunday, he preached a scathing sermon attacking the clergy of Denmark for unfaithfulness to the Gospel. Later on he would have to submit his manuscripts to the police for approval.

Over the years, he mellowed and wrote over 1000 hymns. Besides his poetic skills, he contributed much to education in Denmark. While studying at Cambridge University in England, he got some new ideas and returned to become a leader in the Folk High Schools movement. These were residential schools which carried education far beyond the classroom walls. They made education available at government expense to the families of the poor. These schools stressed patriotism, pride in Danish heritage and held progressive views on agriculture. They soon spread to Sweden, Norway and even in America. The Danes who settled north of Kenmare, N.D., built such a school out on the prairies in Denmark township. These were troubled times in Danish history. Military power and empire were passing. Though "orthodox" in his religious views, Grundtvig was ahead of his time as a folk leader. He had a great appreciation for what was human.

Despite all his talents, Grundtvig was never appointed to any large parish. The State Church was not keen on any pastor who challenged the system. So he spent most of his career as a chaplain in an Old Peoples Home for women. At 78, on the 50th anniversary of his ordination, he was finally recognized. The king conferred on him an honorary title of "bishop." He was 89 when he died.

It's an irony of history that many of the best people are not recognized until late in life or until after they have died. Maybe that's better because it keeps them creative. Praise, while sweet, has ruined many a good person. Today, visitors to Copenhagen are directed to the "Grundtvig Church." Designed like a giant pipe organ, it is one of the nation's showpieces.

I like Grundtvig's views on rearing children. He believed that childhood was "fantasy time," rather than a time to stress reason or emotion. Maybe that's why this poet-bishop, the most Danish of the Danes, kept young at heart. And we still sing his hymns with gusto.

CHAPTER 51

Dag Hammarskjold:
Sweden's "Apostle Of Peace"

WHAT CAN SMALL NATIONS DO for peace in the world? A great deal. That's what we have learned from the life of Sweden's Dag Hammarskjold (1905-1961), pronounced "Ha-mer-shold." According to historian T. K. Derry, he "exercised an influence in world affairs as no citizen of a minor European state had yielded before him."

It was a fateful day in September 1961 when the plane carrying Hammerskjold on a peacekeeping mission mysteriously crashed over northern Rhodesia. The world had lost its greatest apostle for peace in our times.

Hammarskjold, son of a Swedish Prime Minister, had a brilliant career from the beginning. A success at college, in teaching and in government service, by age 36 he was chairman of the National Bank of Sweden. Outwardly, he had everything going for him.

At age 48, in 1953, he became Secretary General of the United Nations, the most difficult job in the world. He soon distinguished himself by securing the release of U.S. prisoners in China (from Korea) and by helping to solve the Suez crisis of 1956 between Israel and Egypt. In 1960, he gathered 20,000 troops from 18 countries for a successful peacekeeping mission in the Belgian Congo.

What kind of a man was Hammarskjold? Usually, we think that such a person must have been an international "wheeler-dealer," both "compromising" and "compromised." After his death, a book called "Markings" was published. It was his private memoirs of religious reflections. Many people found it hard to believe that Hammarskjold could have had such deep Christian convictions while serving in world politics. The manuscript was found in his New York City apartment together with a letter to a friend giving permission for publication. He called it a "white book concerning my negotiations with myself and with God."

Hammarskjold travelled in the highest circles of the world's power brokers. He would necessarily "compromise," but no one called him a "compromised" person, not even the Soviet Union. They did call him a "murderer" and an "agent of imperialism," but not a "self-seeking" dictator.

The truth is that Hammarskjold was a tender hearted person with strong feelings for the poor and dispossessed, though he had never been either. He felt deeply the criticisms that went with the job. Two convictions motivated his actions: First, that a person has to forget his ego to fulfil life's calling as an instrument of God; and second, that the "way of the Cross," with suffering, sacrifice and humiliation, was the price that he would have to pay. In "Markings," he wrote: "Goodness is something so simple: always to live for others, never to seek one's own advantage." A few months after his death, Dag Hammarskjold was awarded the Nobel Peace Prize.

When we say, "Blessed are the peacemakers," we should remember Dag Hammarskjold. He was one of them. Sweden and Swedes everywhere can be justly proud of this man whose kind is so desperately needed today.

CHAPTER 52

Herman Wedel Jarlsberg—
A Statesman To Be Remembered

"JARLSBERG" IS THE NAME OF A CHEESE imported from Norway. It's also the name of the largest farm in Norway, located 100 miles southwest of Oslo, with 30,000 acres under cultivation. The farm house is a castle built in 1701.

In the old days, Norway was ruled mainly by nobles who elected the kings at the "Thing" assemblies. Power struggles between the kings and the nobles were common. After the Black Death of 1349, the nobles and their extensive land holdings were almost wiped out. Then came the Danish period (1397-1814) when Norway was ruled from Copenhagen. The Danish kings would secure the services of German families of noble background to administer Norway for them. This is also how the Preus family came to Norway from Germany, according to Prof. Kris Skrondal.

One of these German nobles was Peter Schumacher, known as Count Griffenfeld. When he fell from royal favor, he spent the rest of his life in prison on Munkholmen in Trondheim harbor. His vast land holdings ended up in the hands of another German family. It was sold to a baron, Field Marshall General Wilhelm von Wedel. He was from Oldenburg in northwest Germany, also the origin of the royal family of Denmark-Norway from 1448-1863. Von Wedel commanded Norway's military forces. The name given to the farm was "Jarlsberg," which means the "Jarl's hill." A "jarl" (an earl), was a rank of nobility next to royalty. It reminds me of a game we played as children called "King of the Hill."

Twelve generations of Wedel Jarlsbergs have lived on this farm. Those of us from peasant stock may not always feel too charitable towards aristocratic families. However, the Wedel Jarlsbergs are an example of a noble line that has rendered invaluable service that was beyond the capability of peasants.

One of the most famous of these was Herman Wedel Jarlsberg (1779-1840). He played a major role in writing the constitution of 1814

135

which Norwegians love to celebrate every May 17. It was his leadership which guided the writing of Norway's civil rights and persuaded the Swedish king, Karl Johan, to honor it. He favored Norway electing the king of Sweden to be its new royalty after England forced out the Danes. In 1836, he became the "Statholder" (representative) in Oslo for the Swedish king.

Herman Wedel Jarlsberg married the only daughter of Peder Anker from Bogstad near Oslo and inherited his estate of 5,500,000 acres of land, plus saw mills, iron works and other industries. Another wealthy Norwegian, Carsten Anker, opened his house at Eidsvoll for the constitutional assembly meetings. The good thing that has to be said about these very rich people is that they championed the cause of democracy while staying on good terms with royalty. Afterall, kings have no money except what they collect in taxes, and the Ankers and Wedel Jarlsbergs were highly successful businessmen. So the next time you pass a cheese counter and read "Jarlsberg," remember that it is a name which Norwegians honor.

CHAPTER 53

Gustavus Adolphus—
"Lion Of The North"

WHO IS THE GREATEST SWEDE that ever lived? There have been many, but King Gustavus Adolphus (1594-1632) usually wins the popularity poll. Though only 38 when he died, he changed Sweden from an isolated kingdom in the north to a modern nation respected by its neighbors. Rarely has one person shaped a nation so much.

My interest in famous people centers on their childhood influences. What made Gustavus such a dynamic leader? He was an exceptionally bright child and was trained from infancy to be a king. By age five, he had seen both battle and shipwreck and had learned to speak both Swedish and German. Under the guidance of a famous tutor, he studied literature, philosophy, theology, music, military science and gained skill in 12 languages. He was taught thrift and a strict moral code. His father, Charles IX, died when Gustavus was only 17, before the legal age to receive the crown. Axel Oxenstierna, one of the nobles, arranged for early accession. Before assuming power, he signed a charter of guarantees for the rights of the people. By sharing power, he gained more power.

Those were not good times. The political conflicts of Europe were deeply rooted in religious tensions. The "Thirty Years War" (1618-48) pitted Protestant against Roman Catholic. No war is good, but religious wars are the worst of all. Greed, jealousy and fear on both sides of the conflict have a way of turning theology into tragedy. Into such a struggle, the Swedish king came to the aid of the Protestant princes of Germany.

On June 17, 1630, Gustavus sailed with 13,000 men. Once in Germany, he was joined by an additional 26,000. What made him effective in battle was the superior training of his troops and the best artillery in Europe, plus mobility, discipline and a faster firing musket. But there was more. Each company of soldiers had its own chaplain. There were

137

prayers twice a day and a sermon once a week. Hymns were sung in battle. Gustavus led the only army in history to have no "camp followers." This kept them free from venereal disease.

On Nov. 6, 1632, Gustavus fell at Lutzen near Leipzig, while winning his last battle. His heart was wrapped in a silk shirt and returned to Sweden. Visitors may see the shirt in Stockholm today.

Important as the military victories of Gustavus are regarded, his domestic policies and administrative improvements were even more important. Sweden became one of the most efficient and well-organized governments in Europe. Oxenstierna guided the government while the king was away.

Gustavus Adolphus is honored in America by a college in St. Peter, MN, which was founded in 1862 and bears his name. His statue watches over the campus.

It is difficult for us who live today to judge the military heroes of the past. But there is no question how the contemporaries of Gustavus regarded him, even his enemies. They called him the "Lion of the North."

CHAPTER 54

Mannerheim—
A Name The Finns Trust

I N FINLAND'S SHORT HISTORY as a free nation (since 1917), its determination for freedom has often been tested. Its most dramatic moment was in the "Winter War" of 1939-1940 with the Soviet Union. The free world cheered as the gallant Finns successfully resisted the first Soviet invasion attempt. Unfortunately, they did little else.

One leader stood out in that struggle, Carl Gustav Mannerheim (1867-1951). The Mannerheims had come to Sweden from Holland and were made "nobles." During the reign of the Swedish king, Gustavus III (1771-92), they moved to Finland. They were politically conservative, aristocratic and were confirmed monarchists. There was nothing unusual about that in those times. The one Mannerheim who stands out as a national hero, Carl Gustav, went to Russia in 1889, at the age of 22, to seek a career in the military. At that time Finland was under the control of the Czar's government. He distinguished himself in the war with Japan (1905).

When the Russian Revolution of 1917 took place, Mannerheim returned to Finland at the age of 51 to drive out the Bolsheviks. The German military gave aid. In 1918, he became "Regent" of Finland and ran the government until a new constitution was ratified on July 17, 1919. Then Mannerheim retired to private life.

By 1931, the Finns feared that the Soviets may try to reclaim the lands controlled by the Czars. Mannerheim returned to public life at age 64 as Chairman of National Defense. The "Mannerheim Line" was built 20 miles in depth, consisting of concrete bunkers, tank barriers, and artillery.

In August 1939, Hitler and Stalin made a secret treaty to divide eastern Europe. In October, Stalin demanded that Finland turn over areas sensitive to the Russian borders. He offered other land in return. Mannerheim advised the Finns to accept, but the government in Helsinki felt confident that help would come from Britain, France and their Scandinavian neighbors. Stalin's patience ran out and on Nov. 30, 1939, bombs fell on Helsinki. Instead of rolling over, the Finns surprised the world and gave the Soviets a bloody nose. The Russians were unprepared for such determined resistance.

Unfortunately, the free world (and Hitler too) miscalculated the ability of the Soviet military. Mannerheim knew better. When a second Soviet offensive began, the Finns fought valiantly before being overwhelmed by massive numbers of weapons and troops. Mannerheim bargained for the best possible terms. When the Nazi invasion of Russia took place, Mannerheim's forces retaliated against the Soviets in Finland, but would not commit themselves to aggression against Russian territory. The aging commander was "Mr. Finland" during those days. He served as president from 1944 to 1946 when he retired due to ill health. He died in 1951.

Mannerheim will live in Finnish memory as a name to be trusted. Small nations need strong people. Long live the Finns in their determination to be free.

CHAPTER 55

Journey
To Surnadal

THE SEARCH FOR "ROOTS" has become a passion for our generation. My quest began long before the eventual journey to my ancestral homeland. There was a problem. We had incorrect information about my paternal grandfather's birthplace. It seems strange that he could have reared a family of seven children and failed to give them such vital information. The record of his death in the state capitol in Bismarck, N.D., lists Sunndal, Norway. A visit by an aunt to Norway turned up no trace of roots there.

A chance meeting with Prof. Kris Skrondal of Norway in 1976 renewed the search. We were seated across the table for breakfast at Luther College in Decorah, IA. Seeing my name tag, he asked, "Where does your name come from?" I told him that it was from somewhere in the Trondheim area. To my surprise, he said, "I know where it is and have been there many times." Then he drew a map locating "Surnadal." I was not convinced, but it was too exciting to drop.

A couple of months later, a letter came from Prof. Skrondal inviting us to his home in Mosjoen, about 300 miles north of Trondheim. We arrived there in mid June 1977. After a visit to his "hytte" (cottage) near Hattfjeldal (in "Lappland"), we journeyed to Surnadal, a valley about 75 miles southwest of Trondheim.

The road sign at the bridge by Per Moen's store in Sande read "Fiske" and "Dønheim." Seeing our family of seven travelling in a VW Minibus, the Moens supplied bananas for our snack. Per took us to a Guest House on a dairy farm where Georg Solem lived. I later figured out that he was a fourth cousin to my father. While we prepared our supper in the kitchen, the Solems were watching "I Love Lucy" on TV with Norwegian subtitles. I had not expected my visit to be upstaged by Lucille Ball.

Georg told me that the main Fiske farm should have belonged to Alf Olsen Fiske (1773-1854), my great-great grandfather. (I didn't even know

141

that I'd had a great-great grandfather.) He told me, "When Alf's mother died, his father remarried. The new wife talked him into giving the farm to her son, Peder." It was news to me. I still had some doubts.

I was amazed at the fine fields on the Fiske gaard (farm). I thought all the farmland in Norway was poor. Above the door of the farm house it stated that it was built in 1821 by Peder Fiske. It was in excellent condition and the furniture was from the past century. Georg told me that he had descended from Peder and that my grandfather, Ole, and his father had been best friends.

That evening, I stood on a mountainside above the valley, still wondering. A strange feeling came over me. It must be the place! A visit to the nearby Mo Church left no doubts. I was "home" at last. The cemetery was well marked with stones bearing the family name.

I could hardly wait to get home and tell my relatives about this discovery. What if the inheritance had not been botched? What if my grandfather had remained in the fertile valley of Surnadal? Where would I be today?

Mo Church in Surnadal.

CHAPTER 56

Visit
To Storen

MY SEARCH FOR ROOTS took our family to "Eggen," about four miles east of Storen, which is about 30 miles south of Trondheim. Our family on my paternal grandmother's side traces its ancestry to the farm's beginning.

When the "Black Death" struck Norway in 1349, two out of every three people died. Most of the survivors fled from the mountains and went to live by the sea. It wasn't until the 1700s or later that much of the interior was re-inhabited. That is why many of these farms date back to relatively modern times.

Such is Eggen. It presents a sharp contrast to "Fiske" in Surnadal, across the mountains to the west. Eggen is a typical mountainside farm. There is no flat land and rocks are everywhere. People took their names from the farms. My home community in the north part of Richland County, North Dakota, reads like a transplant of Storen. Names like Folstad, Sokness, Gylland, Skarvold (Score), Wollan and many others originate in that area of Norway. Another farm, just a couple of miles east of Eggen is Rognes. Members of that family immigrated to Astoria, South Dakota, and have given distinguished leadership as Lutheran pastors in America.

There was a light rain as we drove over the mountains from Orkdal. Fortunately for us, we found a line of cousins across the Trondelag who telephoned ahead to arrange our next visits. Driving to farms one has never seen before can be a test, especially over narrow mountain highways. Besides, there are a lot of emotional energies burned up when searching for roots. We knew, however, when we had arrived at Eggen. Cousin Ole was waiting by the mailbox holding an umbrella and a miniature American flag. He didn't speak a word of English. Neither did anyone else in the household, except for a daughter-in-law. It helped that my dialect is from that valley.

We were greeted at the doorway by Anders, the patriarch of the farm,

143

a cousin to my father. I had been told that he looked a lot like my father who had died in 1969. But I was unprepared for what I saw. He was an almost perfect "look alike." I was so stunned that I became speechless and could hardly look at him. In silence he handed me a picture of my father's family. It was taken in 1917, just before Uncle Olaf went off to the war in France, from which he did not return.

A short distance away was a two-story house built of hewn oak logs, seven or eight inches thick. I guessed it to be about 200 years old but it looked as solid as the mountains. It had been home for many generations of my maternal grandmother's family and is still in use. In such situations, one stands in awe. All of a sudden, the past comes alive in the woodwork, the landscape and in the profiles of the present inhabitants.

If you travel to the "Old Country" in search of roots, it will be easier if you are looking for "place" names. It is no guarantee that you will find blood relatives, but it will be exciting. It's harder if your name is Anderson, Jacobson, Johnson, Larson or Olson. But don't give up. And if you ever do find your ancestral sites, you will have one the greatest thrills of your life.

CHAPTER 57

Discoveries
In Trondheim

FROM EARLIEST CHILDHOOD, I had heard the wonders of the Nidaros "Domkirken" (cathedral) in Trondheim. A picture of this church, the grandest in Scandinavia, had hung in our living room since 1906. My mother had told me that new work on this building will go on "forever." When I saw it, I'd have recognized it anywhere.

It was an exciting moment to see this historic landmark which dominates the city from every direction. Here is where St. Olaf Haraldsson was buried almost a thousand years ago. I was surprised at the simplicity of the worship service, which showed the influence of Hans Nielsen Hauge. Just to be in Norway's first capital, founded by King Olaf Tryggvason (995) and to walk on its streets, was an awesome feeling.

It's in the homes that the visitor learns the secrets of a city. Fortunately, we had discovered cousins in Trondheim. Gunhild Krogstad, a cousin to my father, proved a most delightful host. She served us rommegrøt. To my surprise, our children wanted seconds. In preparation for the trip, we were careful to teach them the polite words of greeting, appreciation and basic survival. My mother had taught them the Norwegian table prayer while visiting her.

At Gunhild's house, we did it up right. To the tune of the doxology, we stood and sang the prayer: "I Jesu Navn, gaa vi til Bords at spise og drikke paa dit Ord; dig Gud til AEre os till Gavn, saa faar vi Mad i Jesu Navn. Amen." (In Jesus' Name, we go to the table to eat and drink at your word; to you, O God, be praise and to us the gift, so we receive our food in Jesus' Name. Amen.) Tears came to Gunhild's happy eyes when she saw that her American cousins had kept the faith learned in Norway.

We encountered two conflicting theories of what is best to do after eating a big meal. In Mosjoen, Prof. Skrondal had insisted that everyone must take a nap for at least an hour. But in Trondheim, the cousins got up from the table and took us on a brisk five mile hike.

One of the most interesting places to visit in this ancient city of the North is the "Folkemuseet" (Folk Museum). It was quite a shock to see some of the buildings which sheltered our ancestors. Cattle and people lived in adjoining rooms. I especially noticed the low ceilings and the short beds. The windows were few and small and did not have clear glass panes. The most interesting building of all is the "stabbur." It is a storage shed built of logs where food and grain are kept and is set on pillars of stone. The front step is at a distance from the threshold. This is how they keep mice out of their supplies.

The visit to Trondheim was returned to our house in Minot, N.D., in the fall of 1983. Four of the kin came to attend the Norsk Høstfest, including Gunhild. It was her first trip to America. The highlight was to attend the banquet honoring Princess Astrid. We learned, however, that such company was not new to her. Twice she had dined with King Haakon VII and King Olav V, when her husband had been honored for his lifetime of service as a sculptor on the cathedral. They liked the Høstfest's musical entertainment too, and thought Myron Floren was the "greatest." I expect them back again.

CHAPTER 58

A Surprise
In Hattfjelldal

I T WAS A COOL AND SUNNY morning when we boarded the train in Trondheim for the 300 mile ride north to Mosjoen. Snow capped mountains and green valleys surrounded our journey. We were met by our host, "Inspektor" Kris Skrondal, the superintendent of schools in the area. After feasting on a meal of boiled salmon, we prepared to travel to his "hytte" (pronounced "hitta," meaning "cottage") near the Swedish border.

The trip took us through Hattfjelldal where the Lapps were holding a convention. They were easy to identify in their bright red clothes. We saw no tourists in this area. Norwegians moved back into the valley in 1823, 474 years after the "Black Death."

The hytte was located in a narrow valley south of Hattfjeldal called "Susnadal." Only one road led into it. To get to the hytte, we had to portage our bags and supplies over a high swinging bridge. Below was the "Sus" river. It flowed with a fierce torrent. That is why it is called the "Sus," which means a "hissing sound." Huge slabs of slate were piled along the banks. I thought about how many blackboards they would make.

The valley was lush green in color and was humid and warm. Above were mountains that looked like they could be climbed in an afternoon. We accepted the challenge. It wasn't long before we reached the snow level. The water in the mountain streams was the purest that I've ever tasted. It had melted from the glaciers above. Then we reached the level where there were no trees, only rocks and wind. We pressed on but soon realized that this called for winter clothes. Snow flurries became a blinding blizzard at times. And everytime we thought we had the crest in sight, a new ridge of mountains appeared. Our son, Mark, made it to the top and planted a stake. I returned below for a sauna and a plunge into a stream that came down from the glaciers. The near freezing water was a shock.

The language of this isolated valley was very difficult. It may just have been the dialect. One day a man stopped by who looked after the hytte in Skrondal's absence. The next day, we saw him again while driving on the road. Another man and woman were with him. Our host told us that the woman was married to both men. That was a new encounter for me. We asked how the community felt about this. He assured us that they were accepted by the people of the valley, but that it was the only situation of its kind known to him.

As we returned to Mosjøen on St. Hans Eve (June 23), bonfires covered the mountain sides in every direction. This is their custom on the night before the first day of summer. They stay up all night and have a big party. We were near the Arctic Circle where the sun made just a little dip below the horizon and soon reappeared.

We have never forgotten that beautiful valley with its torrential river, the swinging bridges, the reindeer herds and strange customs. If I ever get to that part of Norway again, I'd like to see it one more time. Besides that, they serve the best rommegrøt I have ever tasted.

CHAPTER 59

A Short Stop
In Oppdal

TRAINS ARE A GOOD WAY TO TRAVEL in Scandinavia. Not only do they run on time, but the the cost is reasonable. The government subsidizes them so that fewer automobiles will be needed. The train ride from Trondheim to Oppdal is about 70 miles and is uphill all the way. The climb continues over the Dovre Mountains and past Dombas. Then there is a steady descent through Gudbrandsdal all the way to Oslo.

Our visit to Oppdal was an unexpected delight. Johanna Korsnes, a cousin to my father, and her husband, Fredrik, were retired sheep ranchers living on their farm near Driva, about 10 miles south of Oppdal. Two taxis met us at the depot for our ride to the farm. Since taxis in Norway are not limousines, we could not take our luggage along. We were advised to stack everything in a corner, "No one will touch them." Though there was no choice, I was more than a little skeptical.

When we arrived at the farmhouse, Johanna, named each of us seven travellers as we entered. We had sent her our names, but I still don't know how she did it. I was impressed. Looking toward the west from the farmyard, I saw more snowcapped mountains than I could count. It was June 27. Below were green valleys.

We were served a full Norwegian dinner of which roasted lamb was the main course. It was a delicacy. I inquired if they had butchered a lamb from their flock. "Oh no," was the reply. "We bought it at the meat market in Oppdal." "But why," I asked, "do you do that when you raise sheep?" The answer was simple. "We can buy fresh meat at the market for less than we are paid for live lambs." They explained: "It is because the government takes money earned from petroleum and subsidizes the farmers. Otherwise, all the farmers would want to move to Stavanger and work for the oil company." With only 4% of its land agriculturally productive, Norway can't afford to lose its farmers.

THE SCANDINAVIAN HERITAGE

We talked about their "socialism" with its free medical care, university education and liberal benefits to the retired and handicapped. I asked, "Do you think it would work in America?" "No," was the answer, "because your country is too divided. In Norway we are one nationality, speak the same language and are all loyal to the king."

We talked about America too. Some of the family had lived in the States for a while. In all the world I cannot imagine that America has friends more loyal than in Scandinavia. Even though the politicians may voice disagreements with our foreign policy at times, the people know that their freedom is dependent on a strong USA. They are well informed on news from the New World.

Soon it was time to return to Oppdal and board the train for Oslo. The taxis were on schedule to pick us up for the midnight departure (though it wasn't dark). Sure enough, our belongings were just as we had left them. Not a thing was missing or had been touched. It was a short stop, only eight hours, and the taxi fares cost $45.00. But it was well worth it. Meeting long separated relatives, the delicious lamb roast, the view of the mountains and a briefing on the Norwegian economy has not been forgotten.

CHAPTER 60

At The "Presthus" In Orkdal

ORKDAL IS A PEACEFUL VALLEY by the sea, about 25 miles southwest of Trondheim. In the days of the Vikings, however, King Harald I Finehair (Haarfagre)) fought a mighty battle with the people. Those that he did not kill, he forced to serve him, including their king. He went on from there to conquer all of Norway.

Our visit in Orkdal was to the "Presthus" (the priest's house). In Scandinavia, people refer to the pastor as a "prest" or "priest." The Sogneprest (head pastor), Kaare Rogstad, is a second cousin, our fathers being cousins. The presthus in Orkdal is located on the "prestegaard," (priest's farm). The land is farmed by a hired family who live in a separate house. The profits are used to support the congregation.

The visit with Kaare's father, Stephan, gave a special insight into the war years. He had been a railroad conductor. Though life was difficult, he told me that there were many fine German soldiers stationed in Norway and that they were only carrying out orders. Not all Norwegians feel that way. It was interesting to find someone who did not harbor strong resentment to the occupation.

The farm was a special delight to our children because there were horses for riding. It was a modern mechanized farm, but not nearly as large as those in the great plains of the USA.

The house, built of wood, was long and large. One look at it and I wondered about the heating bill. The ceilings were at least 10 feet high. The rooms were spacious, with living quarters and an office on the first floor. Bedrooms were on the second floor, with some of them used for guests. Dinner was served us in the family dining room, not the banquet room. It was a cozy setting with a large round table. We were surprised when the dessert (butter brickle ice cream) was passed around in a large serving bowl. "Butter brickle" seemed to be a special treat wherever we visited.

The church was built of stone and seated about 800 people. American tourists come home with a lot stories about church life in Scandinavia, many telling how poor church attendance is. This is not what we saw. The annual mission conference filled the Orkdal church four times on the weekend that we visited. Among the guest speakers were some from foreign countries. I was impressed.

While Scandinavians do admit to having an attendance problem, tourists cannot really judge the situation, especially in the summer. We don't do too well in America during the vacation period either. I asked about the attendance during the fall to spring season. I was told that in Orkdal it is quite good throughout the year.

There has been a strong interest in world missions and relief by church members of Norway. On the last Sunday of October, a door to door ingathering across the whole nation is taken which amounts into the millions of dollars. To help promote the emphasis on missions and relief, the television stations carried special programs to help bring the message to the people. We learned some encouraging things by our visit to the presthus.

CHAPTER 61

Travelling With
"Holger Danske"

I T WAS A RAINY NIGHT in the Oslo harbor and the boat to Fredrikshavn was late. The waiting room was crowded with families going to Denmark. Luckily, we had made reservations for state rooms. I like sleeping on an ocean liner and feeling the movement of the sea. I even enjoy blustery winds tossing the ship.

The name of the boat was "Holger Danske," which means "Holger the Dane." It's an old tub which many people will not chance. I counted six lifeboats and lots of life jackets. Everyone but our youngest son, Chris, who was 11, went to their rooms. He was determined to explore the ship, even though it was late. We inspected it from stem to stern on each of the levels where passengers were permitted. Many of the younger tourists made a dash to the parlor area and laid down on the couches with pillow and blanket, instead of renting state rooms.

The "Holger Danske" is a proud name in Danish history. It refers to a legendary hero who is sleeping in Kronberg Castle near Copenhagen. His statue has been in a sitting position so long that his beard has grown into the table top. However, when Denmark is in danger, he wakes from sleep and swings into action.

During World War II, "Holger Danske" was the name of the largest sabotage group in the land. About 400 people had been recruited, mainly from the middle class and professional ranks. In July 1943, they destroyed the Forum, the largest exhibition hall in Scandinavia, located in Copenhagen. The Nazis were planning to convert it into army barracks. The explosives were set in broad daylight.

The seas had calmed and the sun was shining brightly when we arrived in Fredrikshavn, a seaport on the east coast of northern Jutland. We looked for a place to show our passports. There was none. Such is the openness between Norway and Denmark. People travel freely between the countries without passing through customs.

After two weeks of travel in Denmark and Germany, we were back in Fredrikshavn for the return trip to Oslo on the Holger Danske. As we said our "farvels" ("farewells") from the deck of the ship, I tossed some Danish coins down to Thomas, an eight year old boy who is a second cousin to our children. Soon dozens of travellers started tossing coins to Thomas. It was a profitable day for him.

The sea was calm as we began our return trip. But once we cleared the Danish coast by Skagen, the breezes began to blow. It's invigorating to sit in the deck chairs and watch the wake of the ship. Seagulls were everywhere. We had some extra lunch along and offered it to them. They swooped down and snatched the morsels out of our hands.

After about six hours, the coasts of Norway came into view. An ocean ride is the most beautiful way to enter any part of Scandinavia. The deep blue water of the Oslofjord, the brightly painted buildings on the green hills and the mountains in the background glistened under the warm sunshine that greeted us. "Velkommen til Norge" ("Welcome to Norway"), it seemed to say. It was a day we will always remember.

CHAPTER 62

By The Sands
Of The North Sea

THE SANDS ON THE SEASHORE have many stories to tell, if you listen and look carefully. Such was my experience when I visited the north coast of Denmark. Exciting events of the past raced through my mind. The ancient Vikings knew these shores well. During World War I, the British and German navies fought a mighty duel within sound of these shores, called the Battle of Jutland. As the Nazi invasion of Norway began on April 9, 1940, people stood in awe to the thundering sounds of the Goering's Luftwaffe (Air Force) heading North.

Today the sands are peaceful. In the long days of summertime, the beach is alive with swimmers and sunbathers. Visitors may need to brace themselves against the shock of seeing those who want a total tan among the sand dunes. The law requires that cabins are set back about a half mile from the beach to insure that the public has an adequate area for recreation. In the evenings, people come out from the towns and villages to walk on the beaches. It's delightfully beautiful and restful. At one point in our stroll, we discovered the grave of Holger Drachmann (1846-1908), a famous Danish poet.

All over the sand dunes of northern Denmark are concrete bunkers left by the Nazis. They are grim reminders of the Fortress Europe built by Hitler's mad war machine. The Danes, however, maintained a magnificent sense of humor in those dark days. They were gutsy too. Since Denmark was not officially at war with the Nazis, they kept on pretty much with business as usual.

One of the stories circulating in my wife's family is how the Nazis bought electrical power from the cities for their bunkers. However, they needed an auxiliary power plant. My wife's Uncle Hans was a building contractor in Hjørring. The Nazis hired him to construct their power plant. Studying the blueprints carefully, he saw that the engine room was just a little too low to allow the pistons full movement. So he built it exactly to specification.

THE SCANDINAVIAN HERITAGE

The Danes saw to it that the city power failed once in a while. When this happened, the Nazi commander demanded Uncle Hans to explain why the power plant did not work. He went with the officer to study the problem. Then he pointed out that specifications had been incorrect. He remedied it for them by chiselling out some overhead room. What he did not tell the officer was that the ocean air had rusted the engine. At the next power failure, the Nazi commander demanded another explanation. Uncle Hans obliged by another inspection tour which revealed the problem. He recommended that they get a big derrick which could lift up the building to install a new engine. One was ordered from Hamburg. It never arrived. This was not the only time that Uncle Hans had some fun with the enemy.

"Deilig Danmark" ("beautiful Denmark") is the way Danes refer to their country. Everything seems to be in its proper place. Fields look like well kept gardens. There is no junk or litter laying around. The people are proud, patriotic and experts at survival. If you ever go there, look carefully around and listen. The landscape has many stories to tell.

CHAPTER 63

"Legoland"—
A Playland For All Ages

A N AMERICAN "WESTERN VILLAGE" in Denmark? Not only that, but the faces of four American presidents, just like the Black Hills of South Dakota. These, however, are not cut out of rock but are constructed of miniature plastic building blocks. Where? In "Legoland," the home of the famous Lego blocks manufactured in Denmark.

It is not surprising to find profiles of American presidents in Denmark. After all, the sculptor who did the Black Hills monuments was Gutzlom Borglum, whose parents had come from Copenhagen. Danes have long had a fascination with America. They melted into the American scene more quickly than almost any other immigrant group. In addition to the American presidents, there are also replicas of castles, cathedrals, manor houses, harbors, ships and even a space launch paid. "Lego" means "play" in Danish, and "Legoland" means "Playland." It is properly named.

Legoland is located near Billund, just a few miles to the west of Vejle. It's easy to find because it is just a short detour off the main highway running between Hamburg, Germany, and the North Sea coast of Denmark. Our son, Chris, had fun driving a miniature car in the "playland." It was also the only place we found popcorn for sale in Denmark.

There is more to this community than a park designed for tourists. Off a few miles to the northwest is one of the most famous landmarks in Danish history. Two mounds mark the burial places of Denmark's earliest royalty, King Gorm and Queen Thyra. Their son, King Harald "Bluetooth," who was Denmark's first Christian ruler, has left a marker written in runic that is over 1000 years old. Gorm the "Gamle" (the "old") was the founder of the present Danish royal family. His descendants eventually became related to almost every royal house in Europe. So you would have to say that Gorm and Thyra were a royalty to recognize.

THE SCANDINAVIAN HERITAGE

Legoland impresses me as an excellent expression of the Danish spirit. It has a "make believe" atmosphere that is true to the Danish heritage. Being a small country, often in peril of powerful neighbors, Danish people work hard but have learned how to enjoy life. Their dreams and aspirations have often been expressed in poetry, fairy tales, art, gymnastics, ballet and music. These all require vivid imaginations.

Legoland appeals to the "child" in every person. For that matter, Danes have a high regard for their children. Elementary school teachers, for example, stay with their classes from grades one through seven. Danish teachers get to know their pupils well and cannot understand why American children have new teachers every year. They emphasize personality development and look for the potential in each child on an individual basis. This is also the custom in Norway.

Since no place in Denmark is over 30 miles from the sea, fresh breezes blow most of the time. These are what give the Danes a good complexion. Maybe that is also why they enjoy such longevity. If you ever go to Denmark, be sure to discover some of the things that have made this little country a delightful place in the world.

Lego blocks.

CHAPTER 64

A Birthday Party
In Denmark

D ANES ARE PROUD OF THEIR FLAG which they call "Dannebrog" ("the Danes piece of cloth"). It has a red field with a white cross and is the oldest flag in the world. According to legend, it floated down from heaven as a "sign from God" at the battle of Lyndanisse in Estonia on June 19, 1219. The Danish arms prevailed. The Knights of Malta use the same banner.

The Danes proudly fly their flag on religious and national holidays. They also raise the Dannebrog when family and friends from America visit or on a special event (Sundays, anniversaries, birthdays, etc.) Such was the case when we visited the Axel Thoresons near Bindslev on our daughter Lisa's 21st birthday. It was a festive occasion. The Dannebrog was raised. It seemed to us that every home had a place to fly the flag.

We learned some interesting things about Danish customs. They give presents just like Americans, but one of their delights is to serve hot "sjokolade" (chocolate). They have a song which they sing while serving it. But to our surprise, everybody went to the living room to watch television in the middle of the party. The "Muppet" show was on in English with Danish subtitles. The party simply stopped until the program was over.

Though Denmark is a modern country today, it's easy to feel that the ghosts of the ancient Vikings might be lurking nearby. Not far from Bindslev, between Vendsyssel (the northern tip of Jutland) and the main body of land is a place called "Lindholm Hoje." Close by is the city of Norresundby, across the river from Aalborg. It was a strategic base for the Vikings. An ancient cemetery with over 700 graves was discovered there by the German occupation troops during World War II. They were digging trenches to resist an expected Allied invasion. Stones, marking the journey of the old warriors to Valhalla (Viking paradise), are still to be found. They are arranged in the outline of boats.

The new faith of the "White Christ" stands in strong contrast to the religion of Odin and Thor, the discredited gods of the past. We experienced the deep Christian piety of the homes in which we visited. In the most natural manner, Axel passed out hymnals and everybody sang. There was also reading from the Bible. One of their favorite hymns is "Tryggare kan ingen vara" ("Children of the Heavenly Father"). They prevailed on our family to sing it in English (from memory). We discovered that hymn singing was a usual happening whenever the Danish relatives got together.

A visitor can only be deeply impressed to find that old values which made Denmark great are still alive. We would not, however, have discovered these secrets about this beautiful country unless we had visited in homes. Where once the dreadful fear of the Germanic gods reigned, now there is joy and human kindness. We met many young people, too, who share these values of their parents. Besides being a "happy" birthday party, it was a discovery of roots, family fun and the Dannebrog. Long may it fly for Danes everywhere.

CHAPTER 65

First Stop—
Ellis Island

ONE HUNDRED AND FIFTY MILLION Americans have European origins. The best known of the ports of entry was Ellis Island, opened in 1892. Previously, Castle Gardens on Manhattan Island had been the place where people entered through New York Harbor. Ellis Island occupies only 27 acres in upper New York Bay. At its busiest time around the turn of the century, 5,000 people a day were processed through its gates. In all, 12 million people passed through its portals to begin a new life in America. More than a million came that way in 1907, the busiest of all years. Sometimes it resembled a "stockyard." The wealthy, however, were processed on board ship and were let off on the west side of Manhattan Island. In 1954, after 62 years of use, the facilities were abandoned.

Most immigrants spent just four or five emotion packed hours on the island. Each immigrant was tagged with a number. Luggage was examined, physical examinations were administered by physicians, called "six second doctors." They were checked for lameness, goiters, mental illness, hernias, fleas and contagious diseases. 250,000 (2%) were sent back to Europe, the most common reason being "trachoma, then an incurable eye disease. Some people were returned because of diseases incurred while travelling to America. Sometimes families were separated here, never to be reunited. Some who were denied entrance "jumped ship."

Ellis Island saw everything. Births, marriages, concerts and deaths were all a part of this place. New York physicians would visit its morgue to study diseases that they had never seen before. Those who passed the physicals, were questioned by a clerk: "Your name?" The clerks weren't always careful spellers and as a result some new names were given out, even though translators were available. I know of at least two Johannson families that were permanently renamed Jones. Other questions dealt with nationality, destination, who paid the fare, literacy, amount of money the immigrant possessed, and record of being in prison or poorhouse. Twenty-one questions were designed to keep out paupers, the insane, criminals, contract laborers (used as strike breakers), polygamists, prostitutes and anarchists.

The food served to those in process was heavy on prunes. After this scary ordeal, immigrants travelling beyond New York would go to a railway ticket office and continued their journey. While the immigrants were being processed, people from the city would stand in the galleries and look them over. It was one of the recreation sports of the time.

Today Ellis Island is being restored at a cost of between 30 and 50 million dollars by the U.S. Park Service. It has been a national monument since 1965. Originally called "Oyster Island," it took its present name from Samuel Ellis, a farmer in Bergen County, NJ. On a nearby island, the Statue of Liberty welcomed the immigrants: "Give me your poor, your huddled masses yearning to breathe free. The wretched refuse of your teeming shore. Send these, the homeless, tempest-tost to me. I lift my lamp beside the golden door." Some of the immigrants found the "gold." Many more are still looking for it.

CHAPTER 66

A "Halling"
Who Showed No Fear

COURAGE AND DETERMINATION have been a way of life for people of the Northlands since the dawn of their history. That spirit of fearlessness followed many of them to the New World. One of these was a "Halling" named Gulbrand Mellem, the first white person to live in Worth County, Iowa. (Hallings are Norwegians from "Hallingdal," to the northwest of Oslo).

Gulbrand built his log cabin on a quarter section of land in 1876 where Northwood, Iowa, now stands. It was a lonesome life. There were no white neighbors for many days journey in any direction. St. Ansgar was their closest town. They waited a whole year to make that trip when they had their new baby, Gustav, baptized.

Those were difficult days for the new settlers in an alien culture. Unfortunately, not all the Europeans in the new land were law abiding and God-fearing people. Some horses were stolen from the Indians by white hunters. The Indians were not about to allow such prairie piracy to go unrequited. A large group of them came to the Mellem farm. They had been told that Gulbrand was hiding the thieves. The Indians dragged him to the barn for punishment along with the culprits. Neither horses or rustlers were found. They put Mellem in the middle of a circle and did a menacing dance about him with knives and tomahawks. The Halling did not flinch. He just stood there with folded arms and looked at them. Realizing that he was innocent, they threw down their weapons and declared him to be a good man. They often stopped in at the Mellem farm for drinks of sour milk and to fill their pipes with tobacco. They remained good friends.

The Norwegians and Indians got along well. It was difficult, however, for these "Native Americans" to distinguish between the "good" whites and the "bad" ones. For the most part, it was the hunters and trappers rather than settlers who got into these troubles. It was not unusual for the Norwegians settlers to ask the Indians for advice on farming.

163

THE SCANDINAVIAN HERITAGE

Hjalmar Rued Holand (1872-1963) was one of the foremost collectors of stories about early Norwegians in America. His book, "Norwegians In America: The Last Migration," tells the story of Gulbrand Mellem and many other immigrants. I checked the story out with Mellem's grandson, George (d. 1983), who became one of the best known athletic coaches in North Dakota's history. It was his father that was the first born white child in Worth County. George also told me about his other grandfather, Ole N. Olsgaard, who walked from his farm near Kindred, N.D., all the way to Alexandria, MN, to bring grocieries back to his family, over 200 miles round trip.

Few valleys in Norway have sent a higher percent of its people to America than Hallingdal. Courage and the love of having fun were their trademarks. I'm glad they came because my earliest American roots are traced to that valley. So if you have even just a little bit of "Halling" in you, stand tall. It's a great heritage!

The Korens
Come To America

WHAT WAS A TALENTED and vivacious young girl of 22 doing in a log cabin southeast of Decorah, Iowa, in 1854? Elisabeth Hysing was born May 24, 1832, in Larvik, Norway, to the southwest of Oslo. But in Iowa, among the settlers around Decorah, she was known as "the pastor's wife," and was mistaken to be only 16. One older woman said, "Why, she looks like a mere girl!" A bride of just one year, she was married to Ulrik Vilhelm Koren, the new Lutheran pastor from Norway who would become famous among Norwegians in the New World.

The trip to America began on Sept. 5, 1853. After a brief stop in Hamburg, Germany, they sailed to New York on a three rigged vessel, arriving on Nov. 20. It took another month to reach Decorah. Then they discovered that no parsonage had been built. They had to live with parishioners in one-room log cabins until the following October.

Pastor Koren, born in Bergen, was only 26 when he left Norway. His pioneer work took him to six counties in northeast Iowa plus two in Minnesota. He was one of the first Norwegian pastors west of the Mississippi. Educated at the new university in Oslo, Koren brought highly skilled intellectual gifts plus a zeal for the church to that newly developing wilderness and was a formidable debater. He served Washington Prairie Church until his death, Dec. 19, 1910. It is still a strong congregation.

In addition to his pastoral work, he was a founder of the "Norwegian Synod" in 1855 and its president from 1894 to 1910. He played a major role in the founding of Luther College in Decorah (1861). Today the Koren Library honors his memory on the campus. He was involved in setting up a Norwegian professorship with the Germans at Concordia Seminary in St. Louis (1859). The Norwegian Synod felt a theological kinship with the "Missourians."

THE SCANDINAVIAN HERITAGE

The church expected its pastors to visit new settlements of Norwegians and to start congregations. As a result, Koren was frequently away from home. This made life lonesome for Elisabeth. She did not, however, sit around feeling sorry for herself. She was a tireless reader and letter writer. In addition to household duties, diary writing filled many hours. These were later published under the title, "The Diary of Elisabeth Koren: 1853-55." It was her way of telling Vilhelm what she had done in his absence. I suspect it helped to save her sanity on the frontier too. While her husband was gone, she'd go walking to look for flowers, bushes and seeds to plant, while watching out for snakes. She wrote back to Norway, "You must not be alarmed if you read about Indian troubles." She explained that the "hostiles" lived in western Iowa, while Decorah was in the eastern part.

Elisabeth's diary showed what sort of grit, love and humor was found in those early settlers. The Korens were no ordinary immigrants. They came with a purpose and have left a legacy that is hard to imagine, including their nine children. If you ever visit the Vesterheim Museum in Decorah, you can see some of it it for yourself.

CHAPTER 68

A Swedish Immigrant
Writes Home

DIARIES AND LETTERS HAVE BECOME a valuable source of information for writing histories. Richard K. Hofstrand has published a fictionalized biography of his grandfather, Martin Hofstrand, who settled near Brinsmade in Benson County of North Dakota in 1883, entitled "With Affection, Marten." It is written in the form of immigrant letters sent to relatives in Sweden. He states that the "people, places, times and events" are real.

The story begins in Malmohus County in southern Sweden, across from Copenhagen. Times were hard in 1882. Work was almost impossible for a young man to find. He wrote: "Too much of the land belongs to the nobility. They own most of it! And because they don't have to pay any taxes, they keep more of the money than poor peasants such as we." This describes the cause of much Swedish immigration.

"America Fever" was fanned by railway agents sent to recruit immigrants. They painted rosy pictures of free land and prosperity for everyone. Immigrants took a large trunk with clothes, food and some tools. They also needed $50.00 of American money to clear customs.

When Martin arrived in America with two brothers in June 1883, their first big decision was what name to take. He said "Hovstrand," but the immigration officer wrote "Hofstrand."

The early days on the 160-acre homestead were no paradise. It was hard work and the tar paper shack (10x6 ft.) was no prairie Hilton. It cost $200 to file a land claim. A well had to be dug and a year of residence was required before ownership became final. Good crops and prices did not happen every year. In January 1885, one of North Dakota's famous three-day blizzards hit. There was nothing for Martin to do but wait inside until it was over. To leave the shack was suicide. Such cold weather (-30 F.) was unknown in southern Sweden.

It took five years for Martin to persuade his sweetheart to cross the Atlantic, supposedly to visit her sister in the same community. It took additional convincing to get her to agree to join his life on the prairie.

The Hofstrands had to make a major decision. Would they be "Swedish" or "American" in the New World? They chose to speak English but never lost their love for the Swedish heritage. The annual Swedish picnic was often held at the Hofstrand farm. Like many Scandinavians, they were great believers in education.

The "letters" from America were often weekly in the beginning. But when family and farming operations took more time, correspondence declined to an annual Christmas letter.

There were tears on the prairie too. One of the boys, age 12, stepped on a rusty nail and died from lockjaw. (I remember how my father used to warn me about such dangers.) The story traces the change from oxen and horses to tractors, from kerosene lamps to the 32 volt Delco plant, and from the buggy to the Model T Ford. The pictures of pioneer days in the book add a great deal of delight. The author has given us an interesting and realistic picture of what it was like when grandpa and grandma began life on the prairies.

CHAPTER 69

The Mystery
Of The "Runes"

IF YOU HAD LIVED IN THE TIME of the Vikings, you might have learned your "futhark" rather than "alphabet." This is what the "alphabet" of the runes was called. For 1600 years, from about 200 A.D. until about 1850, runes were used to record significant facts in Scandinavia. There are still parts of Sweden where people have maintained an interest in this ancient form of writing.

The most famous rune find in midwest USA is at Alexandria, Minnesota, called the "Kensington Runestone." It was found in 1898 by a Swedish farmer, Olaf Ohman. There is no solid agreement about this stone whether it is genuine or a fraud. But it can be read: "8 GOTHS (Swedes) AND 22 NORSEMEN ON AN EXPLORATION-TOUR FROM VINLAND OF WEST. WE...HAD CAMP ON 2 SKERRIES ONE DAYS JOURNEY NORTH FROM THIS STONE...WE WERE AND FISHED ONE DAY. AFTER ...WE CAME HOME FOUND 10 MEN RED OF BLOOD AND DEAD. Ave Virgo Maria SAVE FROM ILL. HAVE 10 MEN AT SEA TO LOOK AFTER SHIP 14 DAYS JOURNEY FROM THIS ISLAND. YEAR 1362."

The characters used to write these words have some similarity to Phoenician and Greek and were usually made with a knife blade. They were used to mark ownership of trade-goods such as bundles of furs and have been found on stave churches, farm markers and memorials wherever Scandinavians have travelled. In the New World, they have been found in Ohio and Oklahoma, as well as Minnesota.

One of the rune markings was cut into the marble of Holy Wisdom Cathedral in Istanbul (Constantinople). Some soldier wrote his name, "Halfdan," (half Dane).

With the coming of Christianity about 1000, Latin became the official language and runes fell into disuse. Later they have been associated in some places with "black magic," oracles and secret codes. The clergy often used runes for purposes of secrecy. Runic was never a spoken language, only an "alphabet" for Old Norse.

The Kensington Stone is 16 inches wide, 31 inches long and 6 inches thick. It weighs more than 200 pounds and can be seen today in Alexandria, Minnesota. At first, Ohman thought that it may have been some Indian writing. So the stone was laid upside down as a doorstep by a granary. Hjalmar Holand, a University of Wisconsin professor, proclaimed its authenticity. There are, however, a large number of scholars who insist that it is a fraud. Ole Monge, a recognized authority in "cryptography," has studied the Kensington Stone and insists that it is genuine. But the debate goes on. I have a friend whose grandfather knew Ohman and was a "believer." Another friend, living near Alexandria, said Ohman was known to be a practical joker. What do I think? Well, not being an authority on runes or cryptography, I keep hoping that some excavator will dig up another stone and will have sense enough not to bury it somewhere else. I do, however, have a lurking suspicion that it just might be the real thing. However, to satisfy yourself, why don't you go to Alexandria and see it for yourself?

CHAPTER 70

The "Varangians"
In The Emperor's Court

IN THE WORLD OF A THOUSAND YEARS AGO, no city was as exciting as Constantinople. It was the center of trade, culture and political intrigue. The Byzantine Empire, as it was called, was based on the belief that it was an earthly copy of the Kingdom of Heaven. Just as God ruled in heaven, the Emperor was to rule the earth and carry out his commands. Byzantium was no democracy, but rather a rigid autocracy in which the will of the Emperor was supreme. It was the dream of every traveller to visit the city which called itself the "second Rome."

The Vikings were there too. They were known as "Varangians," another name for Scandinavians in that part of the world. It was natural that the exotic tales of this city would fire the imaginations of people as far away as Iceland. Anyone who made such a trip and brought home souvenirs was a hero in his homeland.

The Swedes pioneered the travel routes across Russia down into those lands. Their name for Constantinople was "Mikligardur," the "Great City." They came first as traders and later as warriors. Magnus Magnuson calls those Vikings the "super-technocrats of their time." They led the world in metalwork and ship building. They also had a quick eye on how to make money. The modern name "Russia" was actually another name for Sweden. In those days, Russia was called "Greater Sweden." Once having settled in the cities along the Russian rivers and having built others (for example, Novgorod), they pushed down by the thousands to attack Constantinople.

The Varangians came to trade in furs and slaves. They forced the Emperor to give them these rights. It was not long before they had won a place in the Emperor's court as the "palace guard." Powerful monarchs were always eager to hire mercenaries. The Vikings became the Emperor's elite "enforcers." Emperor Basil II, who came to power in 976, made the Swedes from Russia into a separate regiment of "life-guards." Even

Chinese writers, who visited the "Great City," told about "the tall, blue-eyed, red-haired men" that they had seen. While most of the Varangians were Swedes, many Norwegians were also "soldiers of fortune" among them. They were often given the tasks which were not for the "nice minded."

The military had the highest priority in the Byzantine government. Discipline was extremely severe. Flogging and cutting off the nose or ears was standard punishment for disobedience or cowardice, as well as blinding and execution. An unlucky general might be paraded through the city on a donkey dressed in women's clothes as a mark of shame and disgrace. The Varangians had their own officers that were responsible to the Emperor for which they were paid a salary. "Booty" was one one of the benefits of a military campaign. The Emperor took one-seventh, the officers took half of the balance and the rest was given to the soldiers. As you can guess, there would be cheating. The greatest of all the Varangians was Harald "Hardrada." It will take another story to tell about him.

CHAPTER 71

Harald "Hardrada"
Returns

HARALD SIGURDSON, known as "Hardrada," was the greatest of all the Viking warriors. And if he had not been caught napping in the sun, the history of the western world may have been quite different.

Harald was the younger half-brother of St. Olaf. On July 29, 1030, when Olaf died at Stickelstad, Harald was just a boy. Against Olaf's wishes, he laced his sword to his arm and joined the fight. Harald suffered serious wounds and escaped to recuperate with the ruling Scandinavian family at Kiev in Russia.

It was not long before Harald was in Constantinople with 500 warriors as the famed Varangian Guard, in the service of the Emperor. They have been called the "Viking Foreign Legion." This was a Viking's delight. He was involved in brave exploits and gathered quite a fortune through the booty that he collected. The Empress, however, began to suspect that Harald was cheating on the Emperor's share and that signalled his return to Kiev where his loot was stored. Before departing, they attacked the palace and put out the Emperor's eyes.

After a brief stay with Prince Jaroslav, the Swedish ruler of Russia, and marrying his daughter, Harald returned to Norway. His nephew, Magnus, son of St. Olaf, had become king. They made a deal to share the power. Then Magnus conveniently died and Harald became undisputed ruler of the land.

Harald was a large and powerful man. Some say he was seven feet tall. At this time, the king of England (of Viking descent) died. Harald Godwinson, a grandson of a Viking, assumed the rule. The Norwegian Harald, who had earned the title "Hardrada" in Norway (which means "ruthless" or "hard ruler"), laid claim to England. He gathered a powerful force and conquered the northeastern part of the country. He felt safe since Godwinson was awaiting an invasion by Duke William of Normandy in the southeast.

It was on the 24th of September 1066 that "Hardrada" was resting in the warm sun with his forces by Stamford Bridge, over 10 miles from their boats. All of a sudden Godwinson's army appeared. It was too late to retreat and this was not the Viking style anyway. Without armor, they plunged into battle. The Norwegians did remarkably well until Harald was killed. Then the slaughter began. All the English soil he gained was the seven feet that Godwinson had promised him for his burial. It was a terrible Viking defeat and was the last time they launched an invasion against England.

If, however, "Hardrada" had been ready, we can only guess what success he would have had against William's disciplined, well equipped and battle ready forces. But supposing that "Hardrada" had won, our lives would have been drastically changed. England would have come under Norwegian rule instead of French. It's true that the "Normans" were Scandinavians, but they had adopted the French language and customs. Then the spelling of English would have been quite different. Who knows, "Old Norse" might have been the official language of the United States today. The Battle of Hastings, however, which took place 20 days later on Oct. 14 changed that forever.

CHAPTER 72

The Normans
In England

S CANDINAVIANS HAVE BEEN QUICK to adopt the customs of the lands to which they immigrated. Even when they came as conquerors, they became fanatical protectors of their new lands.

The Norsemen who settled "Normandy" in the northwest part of France around 900 A.D. are a striking example of this. "Ganger Rolf," also known as "Rollo," was exiled from Norway for poaching a few head of cattle which belonged to the king. In this new land, he did not hesitate to accept either the language or the religion of the French. And while these Norsemen pledged loyalty to the king of France, they were sufficiently powerful to do pretty much as they pleased.

A revolutionary change in history was made through Rolf's great-grandson, Duke William. Because he was born of a common law marriage, his enemies dubbed him the "bastard." He was unmercifully sensitive about this.

William became a master of war and kept his eye on the throne of England since he had some legal rights to the throne. It happened that the king of England's thane ("servant"), Harald Godwinson, who was in line for the English throne, was shipwrecked off the coast of France and fell under William's spell and power. He was persuaded (in exchange for his life) that William should become England's king. Once back home, however, he changed his mind when Godwin died and this set up a power struggle. Soldiers of fortune from all over western Europe were eager to join William's expedition. For this venture, he had the full backing of the Pope in Rome, with the understanding that the papal tax ("Peter's Pence") should be promptly paid.

After waiting for favorable winds, William landed in England on Sept. 28, 1066, just four days after Harald Godwinson crushed the Norwegian invasion at Stamford Bridge. Sixteen days later at Hastings,

William became known as the "Conqueror." The stigma of his origin had been avenged.

It took about 20 years before the Normans fully subdued England. Their style of rule, according to Winston Churchill, was "frightfulness." They used mass terrorism and made merciless examples of those who resisted. French became the official culture and the Saxon ruling class that had held sway in England for 500 years was destroyed. The new rulers made sure that all bishops were Normans. William was a faithful son of the church, but he wanted only loyal clergy. The Normans were masters at administration and were highly skilled in law. One of the greatest was Anselm, the archbishop of Canterbury (1093-1109), whose book on the atonement is a classic to this day, "Why Did God Become Man?"

England was now brought into full contact with the continent and was no longer an island apart from the world. Then a strange thing happened. The conquerors began to venerate the old English saints and shrines. They were becoming as English as their ancestors had become French. And it all started four generations earlier when Rolf was exiled from Norway because he had rustled some of the king's cattle.

Better keep an eye on the sons of the Vikings. You can never predict when they are going to do something that will change the world.

CHAPTER 73

The Normans In
Italy And Sicily

THE VIKINGS GOT AROUND more than most people of their times. The Danes and Norwegians who settled in northwest France (Normandy) in the early 900s, were soon overcrowded. By 1036, 30 years before they conquered England, the Normans ("Northmen") began a takeover of southern Italy. It had been under the rule of the Byzantines (Greeks) in Constantinople. It started when Norman warriors, lusting for battle, hired out to the rival dukes of southern Italy. In just 17 years, by 1053, they had become the masters of the land. They had an unusual ability for administration.

The greatest Norman leader in Italy was Robert Guiscard ("the Wise"). Taller than any of his soldiers, powerful in battle, unbelievably handsome with his blond hair and beard, liberal with gold but greedy for gain, Robert dreamed of world conquest. He made an alliance with the Pope in exchange for political legitimacy. Assigning his younger brother Roger to conquer Sicily, Robert marched off to capture Constantinople. He might have taken it too, if the Pope had not appealed for help against the German Emperor, Henry IV. The price of deliverance, however, was frightful. The soldiers were allowed to loot Rome at will. He died in 1085 at the age of 70 and has been described as the "first and the greatest of the robber captains of Italy."

Sicily was controlled by the Saracens (Moslems) when the Normans appeared. Roger Guiscard invaded the island in 1060 and became ruler of both Norman Italy and Sicily. Roger II ruled from 1101-1154. His Moslem biographer said that "he accomplished more asleep than other men awake." He was a skilled administrator and business man. He allowed religious freedom to all and was known as "the most enlightened ruler of his age." His kingdom was called "the richest and most civilized state in Europe." It was a great time for building churches, monasteries, and palaces. Art and architecture flourished. Palermo, the capital of Sicily, was the marvel of all visitors and roads were safe for travel.

The last two Norman kings, William I (1154-1166) and William II (1166-1189), indulging too much in luxuries and vices, did not live long lives. Then as suddenly as the Norman kingdom had appeared, it vanished. But to this day, Sicily has not known such splendor. The German emperor, Henry IV, married an aunt of William II and claimed the kingdom in 1194. He backed it up with military force.

What was the significant legacy of the Normans in Italy and Sicily? Perhaps their buildings and art. These are still admired, but they were not of Norman style. They used the best of Greek and Arabic influences. A chapel begun by Roger II in 1132, called "Capella Palatina," has no equal in art, critics claim.

Another legacy has often been hinted at as stemming from the Normans in those lands. There have been some whisperings that the Sicilian based "Mafia" can be traced to the Normans. It certainly would have fit their temperament for family loyalty and organizational discipline. I frankly don't know. But if this should be so, Robert Guiscard could be called the first of the "godfathers."

CHAPTER 74

Knut Hamsun—
Norway's Vagrant Novelist

SCANDINAVIA HAS PRODUCED MANY outstanding writers. The hardship of the land has caused much reflection on the meaning of life. One of these writers was Knut Hamsun (1859-1952), born on a small farm at Hameroy in Nordland, southwest of Narvik. Like so many of his countrymen, Hamsun visited America (1882-1884, 1886-1888). The New World, however, could not hold him. His first major writing, "Hunger," revealed his critical feelings of North Dakota prairies and poverty in Oslo.

Hamsun's greatest novel was "Growth of the Soil" (1917). It's a glorification of the age old struggle to conquer the land and to make a living from it. A rugged individualist with no confidence in the masses or social programs for the poor, Hamsun struggled with faith and cynicism. His views were tainted by Nietzsche, a German philosopher who championed "nihilism."

"Growth of the Soil" won the Nobel prize for literature in 1920. Hamsun's reputation as a writer spread to both Germany and the English speaking world. The story took place in a northern region of Norway beyond civilization. Isak was a wonderer in search of good land without neighbors. He found his place and staked his claim. In the beginning, the only people he saw were occasional Lapps. He let it be known that he wanted a "woman-body" to come and help him. One came. Her name was Inger. She was no thing of beauty with her hair lip, but she was a hard worker and was good for Isak.

The story has tense drama. Isak never understood why Inger always got him out of the way when her babies came. It was only when a daughter was born with a hair lip, believed to be the black magic of the Lapps, that the reader sees into the dread of those mountain people. She strangled the child and eventually went to prison in Trondhjem for seven years where she learned many useful skills and had her hairlip repaired. To everyone's surprise, she became attractive and the envy of many neighbor women for her newly acquired sophistication.

A key person in the story is Geissler, a wondering businessman who took a liking to Isak and Inger and helped them to become the wealthiest family in the valley. Copper mining became the "get rich quick" hope of the community, but it didn't last. The people would have been better off sticking to their farming. Isak's two sons were symbolic of the youth of Norway in those days. The younger, Sivert, became a good farmer and stayed with his father. The older, Eleseus, had big ideas but failed at everything. Finally, he emigrated to America. It was commonly held that if people couldn't be successful in Norway, they could always go to the New World. My wife's mother tells us that this is also what people in Denmark used to say.

After gaining fame, Hamsun settled down in southern Norway as a gentleman farmer. In 1984, travelling between Skien and Kristiansand, I saw the farm. It touched off a lot of thoughts.

During World War II, Hamsun supported Quisling's National Unity Party for which he was fined 325,000 kroner after the war. Many Norwegians, however, have forgiven him for his war time political views and continue to honor him as a writer. Alexander Solzhenitsyn quoted Hamsun in his novel, "August 1914," as saying "The Slavs are a turbulent people and will be the conquerors of the world after the Germans." This may explain his pro-Hitler views. There were other Norwegian idealists who also chose Hitler as a way of stemming the Slavic tide of Russian Communism.

H. G. Wells admired "Growth of the Soil" and wrote: "The book impresses me as among the very greatest novels I have ever read. It is wholly beautiful; it is saturated with wisdom and humor and tenderness." Enigma that Hamsun was, I agree and highly recommend it.

CHAPTER 75

Finland—
Land Of Surprises

FINLAND IS LITTLE UNDERSTOOD by the rest of the world, but five million Finns (Suomi) are very happy to live there. For over 700 years Finland was ruled by outside powers, first by Sweden and then by Russia. But all during this time, they had a sense of their own identity.

One word best describes the Finnish character—"sisu." It really cannot be translated but means "I may not win, but I will give my life gladly for what I believe." This is the spirit that enabled Finns to such patriotism in resisting Stalin's 1939-1940 invasion. It was also the "spirit" which gave them the determination to pay their war debts to the United States when other nations defaulted.

Until 1548, Finnish was only a spoken language, not written. Michael Agricola, the bishop of Turku who had studied under Martin Luther and Philip Melancthon, published their first alphabet book and translated the Bible. The old stories of Finland's past have been preserved in a special book called "Kalevala." Elias Lønnrot, a physician, went back to the ancient "runes" to put these together. They were taken from songs which were sung by people facing each other on opposite benches.

The Kalevala, published in 1835, came at the same time as the national spirit of Finland began to rise. The Russians had taken over the country in 1808 from Sweden. The Finns had gotten used to Swedish rule, but the oppressive spirit of the Czars was too much for them. Even though the Kalevala was pre-Christian, the Finnish spirit was aroused to pride and patriotism. They were ready for their freedom in 1917 when the Russian government fell.

The Finnish people have deep social concerns. Not only do they have social security and medical insurance for every one, but the Finns were the first to give women the right to vote. Most women in Finland have careers outside the home, many of them in medicine, teaching and government. To help with the care of children, they employ "park aunties," who are professional baby-sitters. "ERA" is not an issue in any of the Scandinavian countries, it is taken for granted. It wasn't until about 200 years ago that a Finnish woman took her husband's name and she was not "subject" to him.

Finland is 99% literate and has a high priority for science and education. They have advanced far in the field of mental health. Social legislation, however, costs a lot of money and taxes are high. But the cost of having slums and an uneducated populace is even higher. A low crime rate is one of the benefits of this system. They have learned that survival and prosperity are not private pursuits, but rather goals for all the people. A socially responsible capitalism seems to be working for the Finns.

Finland's nearness to the Soviet Union presents problems. Officially neutral, anti-communism is strong, but its leaders avoid inflammatory political statements. Finland trades with both East and West.

One of Finland's foods is "Lipea Kala," called "lutefisk" in some countries. Not everybody likes it, of course, but its aroma covers the land each December. Some say this is what has made the Finns brave!

Savonlinna Castle, Karelia District, Finland.

The Swedish
Spirit

S WEDEN IS THE LARGEST of the Scandinavian countries, with 173,630 square miles (a little larger than California) and has almost 8,500,000 people. It stretches for a thousand miles and is 350 miles wide in parts. Sweden is well represented in the New World too. During the immigration period, from about 1840 to 1920, 25% of its population left "det gamla landet" (the old country).

The visitor to Sweden is impressed with the beautiful countryside, its productive farms and clean woodlands. About 100,0000 lakes plus rivers and canals are a part of its land surface. Stockholm, the capital city, is a wonderland for people who like castles and palaces. The country's wealth is clearly visible. Sweden has the highest economic standard of living in the world.

Why is this possible? Sweden has not been in a war since 1814 and that was only a border skirmish with Norway. Unlike Denmark and Norway which were involved in World War II against their wishes, Sweden managed to maintain neutrality. It was not without a price. The Nazis everywhere violated this neutrality. Yet, the Swedes gave much needed support to the resistance movements in both of those occupied countries. Swedish leaders, like Count Folke Bernadotte, negotiated the release of many from Nazi prison camps. Sweden also became a haven for Danish Jews in October 1943.

In the old Viking days, Swedes made their mark on Russia and were famous in Constantinople as the Emperor's body guard. In later days, Swedish kings pushed their way on to the continent of Europe and occupied parts of the Baltic region and northern Germany. But since 1809, Sweden has been a constitutional monarchy. Today, the king is a symbol of the Swedish spirit more than a ruler. He has no power except the persuasion of his example and personal charisma. But it seems to work well and the royal family is very popular among the people. Likewise, the once powerful nobility no longer have special privileges. They do possess much of the country's wealth, but are respected more than envied today.

The visitor to Sweden cannot help but notice that there are no slums. On a tour of the old part of Stockholm, called Gamlastan, I saw an old man rummaging through a trash can. The guide told us that he was a "deviate," probably a "wino." She said: "No one in Sweden has to do that." The Swedes, however, very jealously guard their country against "freeloaders." A few years ago, our daughter, Lisa, was travelling through Sweden to Norway, but did not have her return plane ticket to America on her person. The customs officers questioned her for an hour before she convinced them that she was not planning to illegally remain in Sweden and take advantage of their welfare system designed to help the poor.

The Swedes are a friendly people with hospitable manners, clean homes and a feeling for what is right and beautiful. Freedom brings problems too, but they try to keep these matters within the law. Quality workmanship is found in their manufactured products. If you have never been to Sweden, the next best thing to do is to become friends with some Swedish-Americans who have kept a part of their traditions alive in the New World.

CHAPTER 77

A Visit
To Tivoli

A VISIT TO TIVOLI IS A MUST for everyone who travels to Copenhagen. The name "Tivoli" means "amusement park," but it is much more than most people would have guessed. Passing by its imposing entrance during the day, it's hard to imagine what is inside. At night, however, it comes alive with countless lights and beauty.

The Danes love flowers. The groundskeepers at Tivoli not only tend beautiful flower beds, but they also place fresh cut flowers on trees for decorations. They seem never to run out of them.

The Danes love food too and Tivoli has 25 high quality places to satisfy appetites. The visitor can get everything from hot dogs and pizzas to the finest French and Chinese menus. The service is done in old world elegance that is an art in itself.

I've never been a great roller coaster fan, but the one in Tivoli is something else. It winds in and out through trees. Being a permanent installation, it gives the feeling that there is no danger to the rider except the excitement of the ride. Altogether there are 25 entertainment centers at Tivoli with rides and fun for all ages.

Outdoor concerts with the finest musicians in the world perform in Tivoli. Excellent European performers who are little known in America can be heard in this park in the evenings. The people of Copenhagen flock to these programs, while tourists tend to shuffle around to see the sites.

Tivoli opens at 10:00 a.m. and closes at midnight from mid May through September. The schedule of events includes the "junior" royal guard. These are young men dressed up in the same style uniforms worn by the guards who ceremonially guard the queen's palace. These boys consider it an honor to march through the grounds playing their band instruments. Pantomime theatres are also a special feature of Tivoli.

THE SCANDINAVIAN HERITAGE

Apart from the good eating places and the beauty of the lights at night, my favorite place in Tivoli is Louis Tussaud's Wax Museum. Lifelike statues of many of Denmark's 60 monarchs greet the visitor. The clothing styles of the historical periods are modelled. You don't only see Danish kings and queens, but many famous people and fictional characters. One of these is of Churchill and Hitler by a chessboard. One also sees Henrik Ibsen, Mark Twain, Hans Christian Andersen, Mona Lisa, the Snow Queen, Snow White and the Seven Dwarfs, Charlie Chaplain, the Beatles, Humphrey Bogart and "Casablanca" and many more.

The "Chamber of Horror" features some ghoulish figures like Dracula and ghosts that glide through the dark. I took a picture of one. A guillotin, like those used in France for execution, is a part of this maze. Its purpose is to show that horror is a part of life.

Tivoli is really the Danish view of life in miniature. The Danes are keenly aware what goes on in the rest of the world, especially America. They follow our politics closely. There are a lot of things that will seem different to an American visitor, but the cleanliness of this country and the pride of its people are a delight to see. You should, however, try to see it for yourself.

CHAPTER 78

"Wonderful Copenhagen"

ONE-FOURTH OF DENMARK'S five million people live in Copenhagen. The Danes, however, spell it "Kobenhavn" and pronounce it "Kupin-howen." It means "merchant's harbor." In 1050, Copenhagen was just a fishing village. But in 1167, it was founded as a city by Bishop Absalom. It became Denmark's capital in 1416.

What is there about this city that is so "wonderful?" It's a place of both the old and new. Visitors can see the ancient canals still in use which were built as a defense against attacks from Sweden. There seems to be an unlimited number of museums, libraries, churches, castles and statues. There is also an excellent university, a famous "walking street" (Gaagaten) where people come from many countries to shop and the world famous Tivoli.

Near the heart of the city is Amalienborg, the home of the royal family. It was built about 1750 in baroque design and features a statue of King Fredrik V (1746-66) on horseback. Here you can have your picture taken alongside the palace guards who stand at perfect attention without blinking an eye. Their huge bearskin hats looked awfully warm. The bearskins are obtained from Canada. The most frequently mentioned king is Christian IV (1588-1648). He was known as the "city builder."

A little ways to the north of the city are two famous castles, Kronborg and Fredriksborg. Kronborg was built to collect tolls from ships that passed between Denmark and Sweden at Elsinore when they controlled both sides of the narrow sound. It is also known as "Hamlet's Castle," made famous by William Shakespeare. Somewhere in its dungeons is supposed to be the statue of Holger Danske, the guardian of Denmark's freedom. I went searching for it until I set off a security alarm. I quickly rejoined my tour group.

Fredriksborg was built in impressive Renaissaince style and is filled with expensive furnishings. The most interesting thing that I saw in it was the "escape chair." This is where the king sat while listening to people's problems. When things became "too much," he gave a signal and the chair would be quickly lowered through a trap door in the floor to a horse below. Before the astonished eyes of his guests, the king would disappear and gallop away.

This wealth of Denmark belongs largely to its past when kings were "absolute" and when Norway, Iceland and Sweden paid taxes into its coffers. Today Denmark is a constitutional monarchy with heavy emphasis on individual freedom.

The rights of individuals, however, can be abused. Near the center of the city is a place called "Freetown." It began after World War II as a "social experiment" in some abandoned military barracks. About 900 people, mostly foreigners, live in this walled compound which has become a haven for addicts and criminals. The police do not enter it. The Danes are not proud of this blighted area and it does not represent the Danish view of life.

Most of all, however, Copenhagen and Denmark are "wonderful" because of their people. They are handsome, ruddy complexioned folks who enjoy life. Oscar Hammerstein was not just writing lyrics when he put into song, "Wonderful, wonderful Copenhagen." It is.

The Little Mermaid, Copenhagen.

CHAPTER 79

The "Hanse"
In Bergen

I F YOU WANT TO SEE SOME OF THE BEST preserved buildings from the Middle Ages in Norway, go to Bergen. Down by the waterfront, in an area called the "Tyskebryggen" (The German Wharf), stand rows of connected wooden buildings built by German merchants. They have their own special style. As high as five stories tall, they have sharply pitched roofs. Today these buildings house Norwegian shops, but for almost 500 years they represented the dominance of foreign trade interests in Norway.

Bergen is a lovely city nestled around a natural harbor that has been in use for over a thousand years. Even today with all of the modern developments, its natural beauty has been preserved. It is also the largest city in west Norway. I had eagerly looked forward to seeing the museum of the Hanseatic League in Bergen which tells the story of the German period in west Norway.

Bergen was founded in 1070 by King Olav Kyrre to provide a market place for fish and furs. England was its chief trading partner between 1150 and 1250. But then the Germans got interested. In 1294, trade privileges were given to Lubeck, Rostock and other cities of north Germany which made up the Hanseatic League, on condition that they pay tithes to the church.

It began with summer trading, but it was not long before they built permanent year around headquarters. Open clashes sometimes occured between the 2000 foreigners and the local population (5000-8000). The Hanse brought only men and older boys to Bergen and did not fraternize with the people of the city. They were armed. During this time, Norway was weakened by the "Black Death" (1349) and lost control of its coastlands and commerce. The Hanse remained until 1761. In addition to fish and fur trading, they brought many skilled craftsmen to Norway such as tailors, shoemakers, goldsmiths, furriers, bakers and barbers. They also opened up businesses in Oslo, Tonsberg and Trondheim. The struggle between the Norwegian kings and the Hanse centered in the monopolistic practices of the foreign merchants.

The most famous old church in Bergen is "Mariakirken" (St. Mary's Church). It was assigned to the Hanse in 1408 and regular German services were held in it until 1868. It has a high pulpit, sculptures, a hanging ship and is built like a fortress. During the Reformation, the Hanse sided with Martin Luther and brought Lutheran pastors to the Mariakirken in 1526, 10 years before Lutheranism became the established church in Norway.

Did the Norwegians like the Hanse? It was a mixed blessing. The Norwegians needed the foreign capital to develop business. They also needed the craftsmen from the Continent. However, they had one special gripe. The Germans got control over the cod fish trade from the Lofeten Islands which was used for making lutefisk. They shipped most of it back to Germany. You can imagine the physical and emotional suffering this caused the Norwegians. I had always wondered about the unusual appetite that our German cousins have for this "heavenly food" when they attend the Norsk Høstfest in Minot. Now I know. The Hanse started it.

CHAPTER 80

Journey Through The
Westlands — Part I

I F YOU WANT TO SEE NATURE in its rugged best, join me on a trip through the "Westlands" of Norway. As we go north to Stavanger, with the ocean on our left and rocky fields on our right, we see stone fences built between fields. As we get closer to this city called the "Oil Capital of Norway," the land becomes clearer and well built farms appear.

But you haven't seen anything yet. Travelling north from Stavanger to Bergen, we cross four beautiful fjords. Sweaters and jackets are needed. The wind is chilly as we cross the Boknafjord. We lean on the rail and watch the farms on the hillsides. A little later, we go down into the cafeteria for our second cup of coffee and a pastry. It takes about an hour and 45 minutes to get to the island of Karmøy which has the burial tomb of Norway's first national king, Harald Haarfagre. In the city of Haugesund, we visit Olaf's Church which dates back to Norway's earliest Christian era. Journeying further north, we travel on the the Hardangerfjord and across a heavily wooded island called Stord. After more ferry rides, we finally arrive at Bergen. There we visit the open markets by the harbor where fresh fish, flowers, reindeer skins and souvenirs can be purchased.

The ride northeastward to Voss takes us through 29 tunnels carved in rock. Some of these are a mile and a half long. The cost for building such highways dazzles my mind. As soon as we are through the tunnels, a new engineering wonder appears, switchbacks. Here the road takes us over the mountains instead of through them. No roller coaster compares with the thrill of these highways which switch back and forth on the mountainsde. We look downward for thousands of feet before finally going over the top. The bus can't always make the turn. We hold our breaths while the driver backs up a bit and then moves onward. We meet other cars and busses. Someone has to pull over or back up. We're grateful for a calm driver and the Volvo motor coach with its well tuned engine and its air brakes. The most exciting of these switchbacks is

"Trollstigen," meaning "troll path," also called "troll stairs." Our tour guide, a theological student, plays "Ave Maria" over the public address system on these roads.

We arrive at Voss, birthplace of Knute Rockne, the great Notre Dame football coach and stop by his statue. Some of our friends fill up on more coffee. By this time, we are using both cream and sugar as Norwegian coffee is the real stuff. Others go to Goldsmed Hoel's jewelry shop for presents to bring home. We cross more switchbacks. We stop to pet the goats up in the seters (high mountain summer ranches). The goats are friendly and love to be fed tobacco. In the distance is Jøstedalsbre, Norway's largest glacier.

We see people in bathing suits soaking up the sun on chaise lounges on top of the snow banks. It's lonesome up here. You feel like you are on top of the world. To get down, another set of switchbacks beckons. It's wild country. It's the other Norway and you can never forget it.

A fjord scene in Western Norway.

CHAPTER 81

Journey Through The Westlands — Part II

W E CONTINUE OUR JOURNEY through Norway's western fjord country. Travelling in view of glaciers, we arrive at Balestrand, a favorite vacation place for Germany's Emperor, Wilhelm II. Even today German tourists come in large numbers. Across the Sognefjord is Vangsness, the birthplace of Vice-President Mondale's great grandfather. The name Mondale, however, comes from nearby Mundal. It turns out that Frederick of Vangsness married Brita from Mundal, moved to her side of the fjord and took her name. There's a rivalry in the valley today. Both places claim him. It's 1984 and people want to know if we will vote for their favorite son to become president. They hope we will.

At Balestrand we attend an English service in St. Olaf's Chapel. It's a good way to begin the week as we travel through breathtaking scenery. At the very top of one mountain range is a quaint red guesthouse called "Rorvik Fjellstove." It advertises "Kafe-Rom" (Coffee-Room). We drink coffee and sample pastries while sitting on a balcony overlooking the winding roads by which we have just travelled. Two hours later, we arrive at Skei where we buy homemade woolen gifts to take back to America. We save the 16% tax by having our purchases shipped. While eating lunch at the hotel, we visit with the owner, Jon Skrede, who is a member of the "Fjellklang Spelemannslag," a local orchestra which had played at the Høstfest in Minot.

At the end of another day of spectacular scenery, we come to Hornindal where rommegrøt is a part of our buffet dinner. We cross the Geiranger Fjord, the most photographed place in Norway. We see a Soviet passenger ship. I decided to tease our Norwegian tour guide by asking, "What are the Russians doing in our waters?" Giving me a strange look, he replied: "Your waters?" "Yes," I said, "we're all Norwegians here." We spend a night in Molde, Norway's "City of Roses." Then we travel eastward through Surnadal on our way to Trondheim. Please excuse my excitement as we go into this valley. It was here that my ancestors lived near Mo Church for hundreds of years until "America Fever" carried Grandfather Ole off to the Red River Valley of North Dakota.

Finally there is Trondheim, the ancient capital. Unlike the Viking days, its harbor is serene and peaceful today. The center of attention is Nidaros, the great cathedral. It's the largest and most famous church in Scandinavia. Here St. Olaf was buried. Before the Reformation, pilgrims came from many lands to see his gold casket and seek healing from his remains. Under the Lutheran rulers, the casket was moved to Denmark and melted down into crown treasury. The relics have disappeared, but people still come to visit. Olaf the Saint's body is reported to be secretly buried somewhere in the building. The statues of biblical characters alone are worth seeing.

The old parts of many cities are being restored. New modern subdivisions, however, are being developed. There are no skysrapers. We don't have to strain our necks to see the tops. Besides, who would want to hide the landscape?

Norway is a place of endless beauty, but we just hadn't seen its full grandeur until we have travelled through the Vestlands. I hope you can see it for yourself sometime.

CHAPTER 82

Henrik Ibsen—
"Shakespeare Of The North"

A COUPLE OF HOURS TO THE SOUTHWEST of Oslo is Skien, the birthplace of Henrik Ibsen, who has been called the "Shakespeare of the North." Though he left home after confirmation, he is the best remembered of all its sons. A house on the outskirts of the city where he lived is now a museum in his honor and a beautiful motel bears his name.

Ibsen (1828-1906) spent his early years in poverty, but it did not stifle his imagination. When only six, his father suffered financial ruin. After being apprenticed to an apothecary in Grimstad and studying in Oslo, he worked for six years at Ole Bull's National Theatre in Bergen. Only one of his early plays even had modest success. In 1860-1861, he was so depressed by poverty that he could not write at all.

In 1864, Ibsen moved to Italy. Later, he lived for periods of time in Germany. Distance gave better perspective for his plays. In 1866, he published "Brand," the story of a heartless pastor, which made him famous throughout Scandinavia. His greatest early success was "Peer Gynt," based on an actual person who had lived in Gudbrandsdal. Ibsen had travelled through this valley and heard the old timers tell some of the stories about that ner-do-well rapskalion. Most of what is known about him is found in Asbjørnsen's "Fairy Tales."

Writers often do self portraits. Ibsen wrote: "Nobody can put a character on paper without—at any rate in part and at times—sitting as a model for it himself." There was something of both Brand, the rigid preacher, and Peer Gynt, the fantasizing rebel, in Ibsen. His first plays were written to be read and only years later appeared on stage.

Ibsen, however, was much more than an entertainer. He was a protester of social issues. In "Doll's House and "Ghosts," he crusaded for women's rights a hundred years before it became a popular cause.

My favorite scene in Ibsen's plays is in the opening act of Peer Gynt.

Peer had run off into the mountains with his gun to hunt reindeer when the farm work was busiest, leaving it all to his mother, Aase. He returned with tattered clothes and without gun or game. She scolded him with fury but was soon taken in by his story of riding a big buck across the mountains. She knew it was a lie but begged him to finish the story. Then she realized the truth and said: "That's the tale of Gudbrand Glesne, not of you." No amount of tears or prayers could change him.

After a wasted life, Peer was about to pay the devil his due by being recycled by a "Button Moulder." Only the love of Solveig, the woman whom he had continually spurned, saved him from that fate. Edvard Grieg immortalized the story by putting it to music in the "Peer Gynt Suite." Ibsen relocated to Norway in 1891 for the last 15 years of his life.

As I stood overlooking the mountain range where Peer had taken his reindeer ride, I asked my friend, Knut Lovseth of Trondheim, if Ibsen had ever hiked through the area. He replied: "Oh, no. He was afraid of Trolls." There is more than a story in each of Ibsen's writings. There is understanding of human nature.

CHAPTER 83

Edvard Grieg
And "Troldhaugen"

WHEN DENMARK'S FREDERICK VI asked Edvard Grieg who had taught him to play the piano, he replied: "I learned from the mountains of Norway." When people think of Norwegian music, Grieg is usually the first name that comes to mind.

Who was this unusual musician that combined romanticism with patriotism? Edvard Grieg (1843-1907) was the great grandson of a Grieg who had come from Scotland to Bergen. On his mother's side, he descended from the well known Hagerup family. They were highly gifted in music. It was Ole Bull, Norway's famous violinist, who urged that young Edvard study at the Leipzig Conservatory in Germany when he was only fifteen. There he received a classical training.

The music of the continent did not suit Edvard's nature. Another Norwegian musician, Rikard Nordraak (1842-1866), persuaded Grieg to listen to the folk tunes of his own country. He wrote: "Listen to the unclothed plaintive melodies that wander, like so many orphans, around the countryside all over Norway. Gather them about you in a circle round the hearth of love and let them tell you their stories." Grieg did and he enchanted the whole world with these melodies.

To feel close to the music of Grieg, you must go to Bergen and visit Troldhaugen. There you can walk through the summer chalet where Edvard and his wife, Nina, spent many summers. It's on a lake overlooking the Hardangerfjord. "Troldhaugen" means "Troll Hill." He built a small hut by the water's edge where he spent many hours alone with the piano and musical scores. The dampness was not good for his health, but he could not give up Troldhaugen.

In Rome, Grieg was highly acclaimed by Franz Liszt. He was compared to Chopin. Whenever you listen to Grieg, you can hear some notes from Norway's folk dances. This does not find favor with some critics of the classical tradition. One of his favorite authors was Hans

Christian Andersen. He wrote the music to Andersen's "Jeg elsker dig" ("I Love Thee"), a favorite to this day.

Grieg had a definite purpose with his music: "My aim is what Ibsen expresses in his drama, namely to build homes for the people, in which they can be happy and contented." Queen Victoria told him: "I am a great admirer of your compositions."

Grieg has done for Norway what Sibelius did for Finland. He took the sounds of of nature and has put them to music so that the whole world can hear them. In 1949, when the Concordia College Concert Choir of Moorhead, Minnesota, was on tour to Bergen, Director Paul J. Christiansen took off his shoes before entering the house at Troldhaugen. This was his way of paying tribute to one of Norway's greatest.

The movie, "The Song of Norway," tells the story of Grieg. But best of all, listen to his music and, if possible, visit Troldhaugen. The foliage on the pathway to the house is a lush green. Down by the lakeside, you can see their burial crypt, imbedded into the side of a rock. He was a romantic to the end. And if you listen carefully, you can hear still hear the piano playing the tunes of the waterfalls and mountain winds.

Grieg's composing hut.

CHAPTER 84

Selma Lagerlof And "The Adventures Of Nils"

I WENT INTO A BOOKSTORE across the street from the Sergel Plaza Hotel in Stockholm and asked: "What have you got by Selma Lagerlof?" Quickly the clerk pointed to "The Wonderful Adventures of Nils" and "The Further Adventures of Nils." "This book," she said, "is very popular in Sweden today." I bought it.

Selma Lagerlof (1858-1940) was the first woman and the first Swedish writer to be given the Nobel Prize for Literature. She was born in Varmland, a beautiful area through which the Oslo to Stockholm train travels. As a small child she was not able to walk alone. When other young people were off to parties, dancing and having a good time, Selma would stay home with her grandmother who told her the stories of old Sweden while knitting. Lameness, however, did not prevent her imagination from entering into the stories. Selma imagined herself to be matching wits with ferocious wolves and attacking bears. Elves, gnomes and ghosts were all part of the nights she spent in a dark attic room.

Selma's energies turned to writing. Her diary, written at age 15, describes a trip to Stockholm for medical care. Her family was acquainted with many of the leading citizens of Sweden. This enriched her awareness of the times. But Selma also knew poverty. "Marbacka," the estate where she had grown up had to be sold. After teaching a number of years and becoming a succesful writer, she bought it back.

Two books established her fame: "Gosta Berlings Saga" (1891) and the story about Nils Holgersson (1906). Nils was a mischevious 14-year-old who delighted in tormenting the farm animals. One Sunday, he refused to go to church with his parents. Ordered to read the Scriptures for the day and Luther's sermon on the text, he promptly fell asleep. Waking, he saw an elf looking into his mother's trunk. He captured the tiny creature but was changed into an elf himself. The animals now had their turn to torment him.

A flock of wild geese flew over and called to the huge gander on the Holgersson farm to join them. Knowing what a loss that would be to his parents, Nils grabbed the gander around its neck. In the next moment, Nils was on the gander's back, flying the length and breadth of the land. Legends and fairy tales are woven into the story which relates Swedish geography and history. The author's moral optimism won the day. Nils returned to his parents as a humbled, grateful and obedient son. He became human again. In the meantime, he experienced a series of scary escapades. He spoke the language of the animals and they became his teachers.

Nils was rescued by the author from an owl at Marbacka, when she returned to visit her ancestral home. That is how she learned his story. The adventures of Nils is entertaining reading for both children and adults. In a time when the risque, the sexually explicit and sadism are considered necessary for a writer's success, to find good writing done in wholesome expressions is like finding the pearl of great price.

Dalarnahest, a Swedish horse.

CHAPTER 85

Discovering The "Wasa Ship"

ONE OF THE MOST INTERESTING Scandinavian sites to visit is the Wasa Ship Museum in Stockholm. The "Wasa" was built in the days of Sweden's King Gustavus II Adolphus (1611-1632), known as the "Lion of the North." He needed a navy to transport soldiers to the continent during the "Thirty Years War." For this he commissioned the building of the flagship "Wasa." It was to be the most magnificent warship on the Baltic Sea.

Henrik Hybertsson, one of the great Dutch shipbuilders of the time, was given the task of construction. Oak timbers were chosen which had the right curve. Each piece was checked against flaws. At 200 feet in length and 38 feet wide, it was a large vessel by the standards of its day. A 30 foot bow jutted forward with a lion's head on the prow. It was a dizzy 170 feet to the top of the center sail. The "aftercastle" (top cabin) was 65 feet high. Four decks were built into the Wasa, two of them mounting 64 bronze cannons.

Over 700 carvings of saints and heroes adorned the vessel. No expense was spared for this Goliath of the sea. Just the appearance of such a floating fortress was intended to put terror into enemy sailors. The Wasa was to carry a crew of 135 plus 300 soldiers.

On the beautiful Sunday afternoon of Aug. 10, 1628, the Wasa took its maiden voyage from the royal castle through the canals out to sea. A number of women and children were allowed to ride as it passed through the city. The flagship was a magnificent site, adorned in goldleaf and colorful pennants.

Suddenly, a powerful gust of wind hit the sails and the ship leaned hard to portside. Water gushed into the open ports. A few moments later, the proud ship went topside and sank in 110 feet of water. About 50 people perished.

What went wrong? The ship builder claimed that His Majesty had approved the plans. The Admiral had known of its instability, yet he did nothing about it. It was simply top-heavy. There was not enough ballast (weight) in the hold. If there had been, the first row of cannons would have been under water!

Some of the bronze cannons were retrieved with the use of a diving bell in the 1660s. But it took another 300 years before a successful salvage took place. The Wasa was located in 1956. After a very delicate lifting operation, the Wasa broke surface on April 24, 1961. For the past 20 years it has been housed in a temporary aluminum shelter where visitors can see it. A permanent shelter worthy of the warship is being built. In a nearby museum, some of the 25,000 recovered artificats are on display: coins, pewter, pottery, furniture and other items.

The Wasa is housed in warm and humid air to preserve the wood. But even after 333 years under water, it bears a proud look. The wooden carvings remain impressive. Why? Because the tiny termite ("Teredo Navalis") which feeds on wooden wrecks, does not thrive in the low-salt waters of the Baltic Sea.

We don't know what would have happened to the fortunes of the Swedish king if the Wasa would have proved a worthy vessel. But one thing is certain. The grand ship would not be on display where visitors to Stockholm can see it today.

CHAPTER 86

Who Are
The "Lapps?"

THE FIRST TIME I SAW A LAPP was in Hattfjelldal, a Norwegian city near the Swedish border, a short distance below the Arctic Circle. There was no mistaking these people in their bright red clothes. There are only about 37,000 Lapps in the world and they live in the frozen regions across the north of Norway, Sweden, Finland and the Soviet Union. 22,000 are in Norway and 10,000 in Sweden. We later met a beautiful girl in Helsinki who had a Lapp grandmother.

The Lapps call themselves "Samek"or "Samer." The word "Lapp" may once have been a term of contempt. They are small of stature, quick of movement and have a Mongol appearance. Their language is related to Finnish. Four groups of Lapps are identified: Mountain, Forest, River or Lake and Sea Lapps. The Mountain Lapps have changed the least through time. (They don't have television!) They are totally nomadic and have large herds of reindeer.

Reindeer hides are a big sale item in the department stores and in the open market places. If you travel on highway E-6 in the summertime between Trondheim and Oslo, you will find a Lapp encampment near Dømbaas in the Dovre Mountains. It's their way to get in on the tourist trade. For about $35 you can buy a beautiful hide.

In ancient times, Lapps were connected with witchcraft. Viking warriors wore protective leather armor tanned by the Lapps. It withstood the blows of both sword and axe. Lapps were also thought to cast spells and curses on people. One could not be too careful around them. In Knut Hamsun's "Growth of the Soil," a Lapp caused a child to be born with a hare-lip. Cunning minds made up for their smallness of size.

The ancient religion of the Lapps was "animistic." They believed that "spirits," capable of being good or evil, lived in nature. Sacrifices were made to oddly shaped stones. Bears were venerated because they stood on their hind legs and for their assumed wisdom. The "intermediaries" in religion were called "noaides" and used drums to produce seances. By means of ecstatic trances, noaides traveled to the other world for help.

Some Lapps became Christians as early as the 13th century. It was not, however, until the 18th century, in the age of "pietism," that the conversion of the Lapps to Christianity became a serious undertaking. Thomas von Weston, a Norwegian pastor, was called the "Apostle to the Lapps."

In Sweden and Finland, a Christian movement called "Laestadianism" developed. Named after Lars Levi Laestadius, a Swedish Lapp clergyman, the Laestadians declare "absolution" to each another during the worship service. Their meetings become highly emotional. They do not use loudspeakers for preaching as they believe the Holy Spirit speaks only through the natural voice.

After the "Black Death" (1349), northern Scandinavia was abandoned by its regular inhabitants. The Lapps and their reindeer moved into this vacuum and were the only people until the 1820s in some areas. Formerly exploited with unjust taxation, the Lapps are now given government protection and public education. If you ever travel in "Lappland," keep your eyes open, you may see some of these interesting people and their reindeer.

CHAPTER 87

"Maihaugen"
In Lillehammer

ONE OF THE MOST INTERESTING places to explore the Scandinavian heritage is at "Maihaugen," an open-air museum in Lillehammer. Situated on 90 acres, it was founded in 1887 by Anders Sandvig. Born in Romsdal and educated in Berlin, Sandvig moved to Lillehammer because of ill health. The area by Lake Mjøsen in southern Gudbrandsdal is highly regarded for its curative air.

I have seen several fine folk museums in Norway, but none excells the displays of Maihaugen. It has brought together an excellent collection of farms, a stave church, a school and workshops typical of the immigrant period.

The "Bjørnstad" farm had been owned by a wealthy family. The land was cleared during the Viking period (800-1066 A.D.). Twenty-six buildings make up the farm site: living houses, barns and sheds, granaries to store food for drought years and tool shops. There was no such thing as "going to town" to buy what was needed. They made it on the farm.

Two other farms are in the museum. "Odegaarden" ("abandoned farm") had been vacant for over 300 years after the Black Death (1349). It has 17 buildings and is more modest than Bjørnstad. "Knutslykka," from north Fron, was built on marginal land. The farmers who lived there had to hire out to make even a meager living. These buildings resembled cotter's huts.

The "Garmo" Stave church has a special story. In 1021, King Olav, the "Saint," travelled through Gudbrandsdal to convert the people to Christianity. He gathered them for a meeting and said: "It would be a pity if such a beautiful settlement had to be burned." The king's custom was to first use gentle persuasion. If that failed, he threatened with fire and sword unless the people would be baptized. (The pagan kings gave no choices!) One of the converts was Torgeir the Old of Garmo in Lom. He was rewarded with a rich fishing lake in return for baptism and building a church. It was reconstructed in 1921 at Maihaugen with its beautiful stained wood carvings and a ship hanging from the ceiling. At the entrance are "stocks" where "sinners" were publicly punished for lawbreaking. It reminded me of Hawthorne's "Scarlet Letter."

The schoolhouse does not compare with today's excellent Norwegian facilities. But it was a significant step in popular education. The law which made confirmation necessary for civil rights also made schools a necessity. The Education Act of 1739 was a milestone for its time, but did not meet with popular approval. The farmers claimed that children were needed at home to work. In the Education Act of 1860, science, math and geography were added to the study of religion. This is when schools were moved out of homes into special buildings. The one room Maihaugen school building reminded me of Colfax School #5, known as the "Ista School," where I received my basic education in North Dakota.

A 10-day summer program called "Norwegian Roots" is held at Maihaugen. Besides the exhibitions, lectures, handicrafts, folklore and music, they have parades of costumes and guided tours. If interested, write: Norwegian Roots, Storgt. 56, N 2600 Lillehammer, Norway. If you attend, please tell me how you liked it.

CHAPTER 88

Linka Comes
To America

S HE WAS ONLY FIFTEEN WHEN WE MEET HER through the pages of a diary. Being motherless by eight and an orphan at 17 might have crushed many young hearts, but not Linka's. She was a "survivor."

Her diary covered 20 years, from 1844-1864. It was translated and published by a grandson, J. C. K. Preus, in 1952. If I had known what an exciting book this is, I would have purchased a copy before it went out of print. Fortunately, Nora Rogness, a great granddaughter loaned one to me.

Caroline Dorothea Margrethe Keyser was born July 2, 1829, in Kristiansand, on the southern tip of Norway. Her father was a pastor and later a professor of theology. Her grandfather had also been a pastor. "Linka," as she was called, had a good eye for what was beautiful and humorous. She had an excellent education in literature and languages. She loved to read Kierkegaard. More than most Norwegian girls, she travelled extensively and was at home in Christiania (Oslo), Bergen, Kristiansand and Askevold (north of Bergen).

At 21, Linka married Herman Amberg Preus, recently ordained and on his way to become a pastor at Spring Prairie, Wisconsin. The ocean trip took 50 days. Because the parsonage was not ready when they arrived, they had to live in a small and drafty room with a family of the parish. The cultural shock brought many tears.

The diary is a blend of simple faith and profound insight into the mysteries of God. This gave Linka deep humility, endless hope and love for people. As the ship was about to leave Norway, the new bride wrote in her diary: "Hand in hand we go out into the world! Be Thou ever near; we always need Thy help. O Father of all mercies, hear Thou my prayers for the sake of Jesus Christ."

Being the wife of a pioneer pastor required a stout heart and lots of patience. It meant being alone for weeks at a time when her husband

207

travelled to new congregations and to organize the "Norwegian Synod" in 1853. In 1861, he was one of three incorporators of Luther College in Decorah, Iowa. Once in his absence, she had to rescue a calf from the well.

Life on the frontier could be harsh on the women who tended the homes. Only four of her six children survived, two sons and two daughters. From age 27, Linka's health showed the strain of frontier life. When the diary abruptly ended in 1864, she fully expected to die. Yet she lived for another 16 years to age 51.

Linka's life may have been short, but no mother has contributed more children to positions of church leadership among Norwegians in America. Twenty-two sons, grandsons, great-grandsons and great-great-grandsons have entered the ministry, including the Presiding Bishop of the American Lutheran Church, Dr. David Preus. Another great-grandson, Dr.Jacob Preus, was President of the Lutheran Church-Missouri Synod (1969-1981). Besides pastors and bishops, presidents and professors at colleges and seminaries, there has been a governor of Minnesota and a host of daughters who have kept the faith. It was such a mother that the Book of Proverbs (31:28) describes: "Her children rise up and call her blessed." They did and still do.

CHAPTER 89

Going To Church
In Scandinavia

SINCE EARLY CHILDHOOD, it was one my dreams to worship at the Nidaros Cathedral in Trondheim. Having expected the stately "Høimessegudstjeneste" (high mass), I was surpised at the simplicity of the service. It was during the summer and we sat in chairs facing an altar in the middle. We sang hymns the best we could without hymnals. We were too excited to notice them on the rack as we entered. We listened to scripture, prayers and a sermon. After the service, I began to look the building over, but was called back by an usher who said we'd have to return at 2 o'clock for the tour. On a visit in the fall some years later, we worshipped in the main sanctuary and found the hymnals. Even though nobody greeted us, asked who we were or any of those things we do in America, it was still exciting to be where St. Olaf had been buried.

Another time, we stopped with a group at the Grundtvig Church in Copenhagen. It's built in modern Danish architecture and looks like a pipe organ. We came early to see it and wanted to have time for prayers. While admiring the beautiful interior, an usher appeared and told us to leave. The tour guide was warned never to do that again! You'd have thought that we we were trying to steal the place. So we went back to the motor coach and held our service, remembering both Denmark and the Grundtvig Church.

Scandinavians have deep, though private, feelings about worship. Visitors get no jolly handshakes at the door. However, if you attend a smaller church with friends, it is quite different. At Bindslev, a small city in Jutland (northern Denmark), we worshipped in a cordial, though reserved, setting. After the service, we walked through the cemetery, looking up family gravestones and ended up at the pastor's house for breakfast. At the older church in Bindslev, the religious paintings on the walls, which had been covered up with whitewash since the Reformation 450 years earlier, were being restored. These were considered too "Catholic" then, but now are prized for their beauty and antiquity.

THE SCANDINAVIAN HERITAGE

The Mo Church in Surnadal (Norway) is triangular in design and is painted red. The pews have gates and each family knows where they are supposed to sit. We saw the font where my paternal ancestors had been baptized and we kneeled at the altar where my grandfather had communed before going to America in 1892. Mothers of children being baptized wore bunads (Norwegian dresses).

The friendliest service was in English at Stockholm's St. Klara's Church. The pastor was a Swedish-American from California. At the close, we were asked to identify our countries and were invited to the parish hall for coffee and pastries. We felt ourselves to be a part of the church universal.

Scandinavia has Lutheran "state" churches to which over 90% of the people belong. Though financially supported by the government for local ministry, Scandinavians contribute generously to missions and relief projects. There is complete religious freedom. Other churches include Methodist, Baptist, Roman Catholic, Pentecostal and Jewish, besides Lutherans who are independent of the state church. If you visit Scandinavia, be sure to attend church services, whether in the native language or English. It's a part of the heritage.

CHAPTER 90

The Lighthouse
At Lindesnes

L INDESNES IS LOCATED AT the very southern tip of Norway, near Kristiansand. The shoreline is extremely rocky where the North Sea has washed against it for untold ages. At the top of the rock formation is a lighthouse which warns ships as they pass by between Bergen and Oslo.

It was a warm and sunny day when we were there. The wind, however, was blowing a chilly breeze which required jackets as we walked to the top of the lighthouse. To our delight, we saw the SS Norway, the world's most luxurious cruise ship, a few miles out on its way to Oslo.

Down below the lighthouse is a dugout in solid rock. During World War II, the Nazis had placed artillery there just in case the Allied Expeditionary Forces should try to invade Norway at this point. The guns are gone, but the man-made crater is a grim reminder of those dark days. Up to 425,000 Nazi troops were tied down for the defense of Norway which Hitler might well have wished to have had on the Russian front. The German soldiers, however, much preferred Norway, despite the dangers waiting by its roads. Visitors to Norway today can't help but notice how well "Fortress Norway" was guarded by its unwelcomed guests.

Today Lindesnes is a peaceful place where flowers and heather grow wherever there is soil on the rocky surface. On the way down to the parking lot, there is a kiosk, a little shop, where refreshments and postcards can be purchased. There is also a house by the path where souvenirs are available including a certificate that will be signed by an attendant. It certifies that you really visited this most southern point of Norway.

It's a long way from north to south in Norway. North Cape is 1100 miles from Lindesnes ("as the crow flies"). The coastline measures 1645 miles with an actual 12,500 miles when the fjords and larger islands are considered. The widest distance across Norway measures 270 miles.

THE SCANDINAVIAN HERITAGE

To get to Lindesnes from Oslo, you drive over a scenic highway that travels past Drammen, Tonsberg, Larvik, Arendal, Grimstad and Kristiansand. This includes some of the oldest settlements in the country. As you come near to Grimstad, you will see on the right hand side of the road the farm of Knut Hamsun, a Nobel prize winner in literature. The countryside is lush with vegetation in the summertime. There are plenty of rocks in southern Norway, but when you get to Lindesnes you realize that the community is built on solid rock. The road past Flekkefjord and Egersund leading to Stavanger and Bergen has some extremely rocky areas.

On your way to Lindesnes, be sure to visit nearby Kristiansand. It's a good place to buy fresh fruit and flowers as you travel. It has a charming open air marketplace and a stately cathedral right in the town square. It's a few more miles and takes a couple of hours to visit this scenic place, but it is well worth it. Brave warriors and kings have climbed these paths. If you close your eyes for a moment, you can almost imagine that these mighty men have come back for another look at the beautiful ocean that glistens in the sun. You'll never forget it.

CHAPTER 91

Hans Egede—
"Apostle To Greenland"

SOMETIMES THE QUESTIONS of little boys drive them to adventures that no one could have imagined. Such was the case of Hans Egede ("Eg-gi-der"). He was born Jan. 31, 1684, at Harstad, on an island off the northwest coast of Norway. Hans' father, the Resident Magistrate of the district, had grown up in a parsonage in Denmark.

Life on the island was hard, but it proved a good training ground for Hans' future. Though his parents were desperately poor, they managed to send him to the university in Copenhagen. Norway didn't get a university until 1813. He loved history, mathematics and astronomy, and had an aptitude for languages. Combining a fierce determination to learn and a stubbornness that refused to quit what he began, Hans graduated in just 18 months and was ordained before his 20th birthday.

After his wedding to Gertrud Rasch, Hans was assigned to a little fishing village in the Lofoten Islands. There he remembered stories from childhood about the Norsemen who had settled Greenland 700 years earlier during the days of Leif Erikson. It had been almost 300 years since there had been contact. Were any of them still alive? Hans had to find out. An "inner Voice" told him to go to Greenland and search.

It took 13 years before Hans got the backing of King Fredrik IV and a group of Bergen merchants who wanted to trade with the Eskimos. The war between Denmark and Sweden could spare no ships or money for the expedition. To prepare for his work as explorer, colonizer and missionary, Hans gathered information on Greenland by talking to sailers.

For 15 arduous years Hans labored on the west coast of that ice covered island. It was not easy. He won the confidence of the Eskimos, but the "angokoks" (witch doctors) plotted to kill him. Hans called their bluff and put them out of business. He found ruins of ancient Norse settlements, but no trace of the people. Because the Dutch traders

213

burned down one of his settlements and threatened death to Danes, troops were sent from Denmark. This did not prove to be a blessing. Quarreling and drunkenness got the best of them during the long winters. Sometimes they nearly starved before the supply ships arrived in the summer.

Hans began Christian work among the natives and set up trade in furs, whale oil and fish. The hard winters, however, claimed Gertrud's life. Eventually, Hans returned to Denmark where he was in charge of a school to train missionaries for Greenland. He turned down the offer to be bishop of Trondheim. His two sons took over the missionary and trading work and his two daughters married pastors in Denmark.

In Godthaab ("good hope"), the capital of Greenland, a towering statue of Egede stands on a hill overlooking the city. Hans has been called the "Apostle to Greenland" and his family is still dearly loved by the Eskimos. Each time I've flown past Greenland, my eyes have strained for the settlements started by Egede. But from 40,000 feet in the air, all one can see is water and ice. Maybe some day I can pay my respects in person.

CHAPTER 92

Harald "Haarfagre"—
The King Who United Norway

WHEN SELMER NORGARD of Hartland, N.D., told me at the Norsk Høstfest that he was descended from King Harald "Haarfagre" (872-930), it opened up quite a conversation. For evidence, his sisters, Helga Anderson of Voltaire, N.D., and Grace Brietzke of Minot, N.D., brought me the family tree which shows that they are 33rd generation from the famous ruler.

Who was this Harald and how did he become king? He was descended from the royal family of Sweden called the "Ynglings" who claimed lineage from "Yngvi-Frey," one of the Norse gods. At his father's death, Harald became king at age 10 in an area around Oslo.

When Harald became a "Viking," he discovered a beautiful maiden in Valders named Gyda. He sent his men to fetch her for his harem, thinking she would be honored to accept. Gyda, however, was as proud as she was handsome. She said she would not "waste her maidenhood" on a king with such a tiny kingdom and would not even be his wife! She asked why Norway could not have great kings like Denmark and Sweden and replied that she would only marry him if he were ruler of all Norway.

Her arrogance was reported to the king who accepted it as a challenge. He vowed not to cut his hair until he subdued the whole land. He set out at once to conquer every valley and all the coastal regions. It was profitable too, as he demanded taxes and inheritance right from the farmers.

It was no wonder that people fled Norway to settle in Iceland under his rule. Over each of the territories, he set a "jarl" (an earl) to administer his laws and collect taxes. The jarl kept one-third of the taxes out of which he paid his "enforcers." It was so profitable that the politicians of Norway flocked to Harald. They could make more money working for him as jarls than kings had previously made.

Harald's last great battle was at Hafrsfjord, just west of Stavanger.

His military campaigns cleaned up much of the piracy that had plagued the coastlands. After 10 years, the battles were won and he turned his attention again to Gyda. But first he got a haircut from his best friend, Ragnvald ("Ronald" in English), Earl of More. The Earl took one look at the king and declared "haarfagre" ("beautiful and thick hair!"). When the messengers came to Gyda the second time, she accepted his offer and bore him five children.

Harald soon became a rich man and added more wives. He divorced nine of them, however, to marry the daughter of King Erick of Jutland (Denmark). She was known as "Ragnhild the Mighty" and had a son known as "Eric Blood-Ax." No one ever accused King Harald of being "soft." Even to his best friends he gave no concessions. Ragnvald's son, "Ganger" Rolf, was banished from Norway for poaching some of the king's cattle. Rolf (Rollo) went on to conquer Normandy in France. Both Olaf Tryggvason and Olaf Haraldsson (the "saint") descended from Harald as does the present royal family of Norway, including Crown Prince Harald.

The next time Norway's royal family comes to the Høstfest in Minot, I hope they will take time to get acquainted with their 33rd cousins.

CHAPTER 93

"Up In
The Seters"

THE CLOSEST PLACE YOU CAN GET to heaven in Norway is up in a "seter" (pronounced "say-ter"). It is not, however, to be confused with the "Garden of Eden." The seter is a "summer cheese farm" located in the mountains. A third of the farmers used to have seters.

Farms in Norway are usually small, sometimes less than 10 acres of tilled land. Only a few are really large. A hundred acres is a good sized operation. But often attached to the basic acreage, where the farm buildings are located, is an outlying pasture and woods. These also provide a place for hunting and fishing.

In the past, children and old women stayed up in the seter with the cattle, sheep and goats from early spring until freeze-up. This was before school attendance was compulsory. It was a lonesome life and there was plenty of time to think, usually about home. They would also put up hay. There would be a little cottage or chalet called a "hytte" (pronounced "hitta") for shelter and a "stabbur" (pronounced "stah-bur") for storing cheese, butter and supplies. The stabbur is an unusual looking building set on rock pillars to keep out the rodents.

Seters were previously used only in the summer for grazing farm animals, but today skiers come for winter holidays and especially at Easter. Now that there are good roads, snow removal equipment and snowmobiles, the seters have become very popular. But make no mistake, it can be chilly up there in the winter, 40 below or colder. Even in summertime, you'll be glad if you brought a warm woolen sweater, especially in the evenings.

It's an eerie feeling to be up so high. When travelling in Norway, you are either going up or down and usually there are mountains hovering above. Almost everything is below when you are in the seter country.

These summer pastures are usually owned by a group of farmers down in the valleys. Since grass seeding began only about 200 years ago, it was required to have these outfarms. Farmers were not allowed to keep flocks at home during the summer. That would use up the winter supplies. They still guard every blade of grass growing by the buildings. I was going to see the house in Surnadal where my great-grandmother had lived. Eager to get there, I started walking across the field. My host quickly called me back and said we had to follow the road. All the grass is saved to feed flocks and herds.

We saw some large goatherds up in the summer pastures and signs advertising "geitost" (goat cheese). Some of the people in our group wouldn't miss a chance to eat it, while others simply couldn't appreciate its taste. These summer pastures are an old way of life in Norway, but now many of them are returning to nature.

If you ever visit Norway, be sure to allow some time to travel through these highlands. Then listen to Ole Bull's "Seterjentens Sondag," a song of the "Seter Girl's Sunday:" You'll hear her sing: "I gaze on the sun, it mounts in the skies, the hour now for church time is nearing. Ah! would I were home, amid all I prize, with the folk on the highway appearing." She yearned for the church bells, but only heard cowbells. She was lonesome and it would be a long time till freeze-up.

CHAPTER 94

Stockholm's
"Storkyrkan"

"STOR-KYRKAN" MEANS "THE BIG CHURCH." That's what people in Stockholm, Sweden, call St. Nicholas' Cathedral, the oldest parish church in the city. Begun about 1250, it was the only parish church in the city for almost 400 years, except for monastery chapels.

Stockholm is a city of 14 islands, 40 bridges and many beautiful canals. The cathedral is located next to the royal palace in "Gamla Stan" ("old town"). The streets are so narrow at places that you can touch the buildings on both sides as you walk through. Visiting this island is a must for every tourist to Sweden's capital city. Selma Lagerlof, the famed Swedish novelist, called Stockholm "the city that floats on water."

Surrounded by the palace and other royal buildings, Storkyrkan has witnessed many of Sweden's most important events, including the coronations of its kings and queens, royal weddings and funerals. Coronations, however, are no longer held in Sweden, as they are considered too expensive.

Come inside this great church with me for a closer look. It has five aisles. About half way up the middle aisle is the high pulpit. It's almost 300 years old and is adorned with works of art. I was impressed with the heavy overlay of gold and the hour glass which the preacher flips over when he begins the sermon. He stops preaching when all the sand has run through.

Right across the aisle from the pulpit is the burial place of Olaus Petri (d. 1552), who brought the Lutheran Reformation to Sweden. There is also a memorial to Archbishop Nathan Soderblom, one of Sweden's best known churchmen.

The most interesting statue in the cathedral is of St. George, a very popular saint of the Middle Ages. The legends tell us that he was a knight in Cappadocia (Asia Minor). One day he came to a town in Libya

219

where a dragon was terrorizing the people. Each day they had to feed it two sheep. When they ran out of sheep, the dragon demanded humans to eat. Victims were chosen by lots. St. George arrived on the day the lot fell on the king's only daughter. Hearing of her danger, he rode to her rescue.

Capturing the beast, he led it back into the city. When the royal family and the people agreed to become Christians, he killed the dragon. Knight George was martyred by the Emperor Diocletion (about 303). After his death, many miracles were claimed to have been worked in his name. The statue of St. George, protector of Sweden, was erected to celebrate a Swedish victory over the Danes in 1471. Our guide told us that the Princess' statue represented Sweden and the dragon was Denmark. At that time, Denmark ruled over both Norway and Sweden.

There are many more interesting things to see in Storkyrkan, including a huge painting of the Crucifixion above the altar and a beautifully carved crucifix. What especially interested me, however, was a large wrought iron globe representing Swedish foreign missions. When people make donations to missions, they light a candle to repesent their gift. It was well lit. The next time I visit the cathedral, I'm going to light a candle too.

CHAPTER 95

Prince Eugen's
Island

EVERYONE HAS A DAY THAT IS REMEMBERED with some special nostalgia. One of the most delightful days I have spent was in Stockholm on a Sunday afternoon in August. The sunshine was beautiful and the temperature was perfect. Together with Paul Kemper, my wife and I strolled from the Sergel Plaza Hotel to the waterfront. We looked at statues in the parks, including one of the famous inventor, John Ericsson, who designed the U.S. Monitor of Civil War fame. Then we took a ride on a motor launch through the canals. It is these waterways that have given Stockholm the name "Venice of the North."

We docked in front of the royal palace when the changing of the guard was taking place. These honorary guards all looked seven feet tall in their uniforms. There were hundreds of sailboats and motor launches out that afternoon. A couple of stops later, we parted company with Paul and got off the boat at Waldemarsudde, popularly known as "Prince Eugen's Island." It's a natural paradise. There are magnificent flower gardens, statues, a museum and a view of Stockholm that is unequalled.

We found a park bench in the shade overlooking the harbor and ate our picnic lunch. Across the canal was an ocean liner loading for the 16-hour trip to Helsinki, Finland. Time limitations ruled out that ride for us. It was to come a year later. The panorama included castles, church spires, department stores and miles of harbors and shoreline. There was just enough wind to move the sailboats along at a good speed in and out of the paths traversed by motorized boats.

My curiosity, however, got the best of me. Who was this Prince Eugen (1865-1947)? What was the story behind the stately castle and the museum on this island? And why was it named after him? He was the youngest son of Oscar II, who was King of Sweden from 1872-1907. Having no expectation of royal sucession, Prince Eugen became a great artist and a collector of art.

THE SCANDINAVIAN HERITAGE

One has to try to have some feeling for a prince who can never hope to become king. What should he do? To appreciate Prince Eugen, you also need to get acquainted with his talented and industrious friends, many of whom became quite famous. There were an unusual number of noted Swedish artists and writers at at that time. Their pattern was to go to the Continent, especially France, to study. They were often given financial support by the government for their studies. These artists were deeply in love with their native land.

Among them were Carl Larsson, Bruno Liljeforst, Gustav Fjaestad and Anders Zorn. Another brilliant artist of the times was Carl Milles, famous for his sculptures. One of these, called "Meeting of the Waters," is on Market Street in front of the historic St. Louis (Missouri) train depot. It pictures the meeting of the Missouri and Mississippi rivers.

After considerable time in Germany, Austria and France, Prince Eugen returned to Sweden where he became famous for his artistic skills. He was very popular and greatly loved by everybody in the country. I learned a lot from this boat ride and can hardly wait for the next one.

222

CHAPTER 96

The Wild
Adventures Of Knute

K NUT THE GREAT, THE DANISH KING of England (1016-1035), would be proud of his namesake from Spring Grove, Minnesota. Knute Lee, now of Seattle, has published his book entitled "Survivor: Knute's Wild Story."

Even as a little boy, Knute couldn't stay away from danger. A gravestone fell on him at age four, killing his playmate. At age five, he teased a team of horses into a runaway. He missed death from a dynamited tree stump by seconds when 10. It's a wonder he ever survived childhood.

More near brushes with death followed him through high school and at Luther College in Decorah, Iowa, where he majored in music. While teaching school in Glasgow, Montana, Knute volunteered to be a Navy pilot and got his wings and commission in August 1942. He flew patrol planes, seaplanes, dive bombers and fighters in the war.

Knute's most bitter taste of war was off Noumea, New Caledonia, in the South Pacific. A Japanese submarine was sighted and surfaced by an American patrol plane. Out of bombs and with limited fuel, it ducked bullets from the sub until "Ace," as they called him, arrived to finish the task.

Then something unexpected happened. He thought about the 100 men who died on the bottom of the sea. He saw the faces of Japanese fathers and mothers, of sisters and wives of the sailors who perished. A deeply committed Christian, Knute grieved for their souls. The oil slick on the surface confirmed his feelings.

Dangerous landings, impossible formations and high risk carrier take-offs were a continuing part of Knute's saga. But the sub sinking on Aug. 19, 1943, continued to haunt him. About this time, Knute decided to enroll at seminary when the war was over. He graduated from Luther Theological Seminary in St. Paul, Minnesota, and was ordained in August 1948.

223

In 1946, Knute met and married Shirley Foster of New Rockford, N.D., then a nursing student at Fairview Hospital in Minneapolis. I knew Shirley from college at Concordia in Moorhead, Minnesota. Later I was pastor to her family in New Rockford. I had heard about Knute's wartime exploits and wondered how a quiet girl like Shirley would survive his exciting lifestyle. She has done well, earning a degree from Luther College while rearing four sons.

Besides working on farms, railroad, driving truck and cabs, and being a dance band musician, Knute earned a doctorate from Columbia University and Union Seminary in New York. He has also been a teacher in high school, college, seminary, and a chaplain at the Air Force Bace at Thule, Greenland. Now he teaches part-time at the Seattle Lutheran Bible Institute. Even having reached the age of 70, Ace is still going strong, running the half mile in 2:29 at the University of Washington's Master's Track and Field Meet.

ABC-TV has done a movie on his World War II career. Besides the Silver Star for "conspicious heroism," he proudly displays the Distinguished Flying Cross for "gallantry and intrepidity in action." There is no doubt about it, this Norwegian boy from Spring Grove would have done old King Knut proud. They would have liked each other.

CHAPTER 97

Georg Sverdrup—
"Apostle Of Freedom"

THE NAME "SVERDRUP" was synonymous with "freedom" in 19th century Norway. The Sverdrups had come from Slesvig (south Denmark) in the 17th century and supplied a long line of able leaders. It's not surprising that when Georg Sverdrup (1848-1907) came to America in 1874 that he took with him the family passion for human rights. His grand-uncle, another Georg Sverdrup, was president of the Constitutional Convention at Eidsvoll in 1814. An uncle, Johan Sverdrup, whose statue stands by the parliament building, was leader of the People's Party and prime minister. His father, Harald U. Sverdrup, was a pastor at Balestrand and a member of parliament for 22 years.

Norway has a history of concern for the rights of people. Even in pre-Christian times, no man could legally be king without popular consent and kings were subject to the law of the land. The pastors in the state church, being royal officials, were often aristocratic, proud and domineering. The blame for this, according to Sverdrup, lay in the educational system which alienated theological students from the people they were supposed to serve.

After studying in Oslo and Paris, Sverdrup spent time in Germany, Italy and England before coming to America to become a professor and later president of Augsburg College and Seminary in Minneapolis. His two main concerns for the immigrant congregations were to have clergy who were educated for service in the New World (not Norway!) and to have "living congregations" that were geared for mission work. He wanted pastors and lay members to share in the administration of the church's work, neither dominating the other. This was a new vision for the immigrants.

Sverdrup was a champion of the public schools and believed firmly in the separation of church and state. He held that education should integrate life's experiences with academic learning. Concerned for the health of congregations in America, he wrote: "The king does not have the right to appoint pastors in a foreign country . . . only the congregation has the right to call pastors."

Zeal for freedom, unfortunately, took Sverdrup out of the mainstream of Norwegian congregations. In 1897, he and a group called the "Friends of Augsburg" organized the Lutheran Free Church. They feared that denominational ownership of Augsburg would threaten the freedom of congregations by preparing pastors who were not properly trained for work in America. Prof. Warren Quanbeck lamented this schism, stating that allied with such men as J. N. Kildahl, Sverdrup's insight and eloquence could have produced "a healthier evangelism and a more ecumenical and open churchmanship." He claimed Sverdrup to be "almost a century ahead of his time."

I discovered a connection between Sverdrup and Bethany Lutheran Church in Minot where I have served as pastor since 1974. One of Sverdrup's Augsburg professors, John Blegen, gathered a group of Norwegian immigrants in July 1886 to form Bethany.

To my further surprise, I learned that Jacob Sverdrup, brother of Georg and cabinet minister for Church and Education, married into my wife's family in 1860 back in Denmark. It's a small world.

CHAPTER 98

The "Resistance Museum" In Copenhagen

A LIGHT MIST WAS FALLING when we landed at the Copenhagen airport. Our tour guide had a full schedule of places for us to visit. I insisted, however, that we had to see Denmark's Resistance Museum. She was both surprised and delighted. Foreign visitors usually miss the museum which records the dark days of 1940-1945.

If ever any country took literally the words of the prophet, "They shall beat their swords into plowshares," it was Denmark. Once a warring people, the Danes had followed the ways of peace for a century when World War II began. They cut their armed forces from 30,000 to 15,000 and signed a non-aggression pact with Hitler as proof of their neutrality.

Sabotage activities stepped up during 1943. The British threatened to bomb the factories that produced materials for Germany. Wishing to protect their own people from these bombs, the Danes responded vigorously. The Resistance Museum is the record of how with little more than their courage and wits, they opposed a highly organized and mechanized enemy.

Seventy-three exhibit cases tell the story how the Danes joined hands with the Allied forces. Many Danes, trained in England, were dropped by parachute into Denmark to become Resistance leaders. Unfortunately, there were "informers" who betrayed many of them to the enemy. Traitors were dealt swift justice when discovered. Secret wireless operators received news from the free world. The underground newspapers kept the people informed.

One display shows how railroad tracks were dynamited. 40,000 enemy troops were tied down in Jutland to guard them. They failed. We saw a prison cell with room for one person which housed four. There are pictures of Danes who fled to Sweden. 20,000 people were relocated in Sweden which provided schools for children and jobs for adults. Five Danish army battalions were formed in exile.

On Aug. 29, 1943, the Nazis changed their policy for Denmark. Despite their need for Danish agricultural products, they began treating the Danes as enemies rather than as reluctant allies. Curfews and martial law prevailed until the end of the war. Then came the crack-down on Danish Jews, previously protected. Most of them escaped to Sweden. Babies were given sleeping pills so that they would not cry during the escapes.

Pictures and displays of the war years included the prison camps, homemade radios, an arms workshop where guns and explosives were made, scenes from the islands of Bornholm and Greenland. There are also exhibits of the Danish Nazi organization which cooperated with the enemy. I learned a lot.

Our guide told us that her husband had been the head of a Resistance group called "Danne Virke." He had been imprisoned in Germany until near the end of the war when a caravan of "White Busses," organized by Folke Bernadotte of Sweden, brought him home. The effects of malnutrition caused a premature death.

The Danish government has special educational programs to remind the youth about those years. They want them to remember that "eternal vigilance is the price of freedom."

CHAPTER 99

King Olaf
Tryggvason

BEFORE WE JUDGE THE MAN, we should ask about the boy. This is especially true in the case of Olaf Tryggvason (968-1000), king of Norway from 996 to 1000. He was ruler for only four years, but left his mark on the nation forever.

Olaf's father, Tryggve, king of a small area, was murdered by a relative in a power struggle. His mother, Astrid, fled for her life to Sweden, pursued by enemies. Olaf was born on the journey. Finding that they were not safe in Sweden, Astrid set out for Russia with Olaf (now three) to a relative in the service of King Vladimir (Valdemar) at Kiev.

Attacked on the way by Vikings from Estonia, Olaf was kidnapped and sold as a slave. Six years later, an older cousin in the employ of the king spotted him in a marketplace and bought him. Olaf grew up tall, powerful and handsome. In a few years, he was an officer in the Russian army. The other officers, however, became jealous of his popularity and rapid promotions. Realizing his danger, Olaf left Russia. To conceal his identity, he called himself "Ole" and told people that he was Russian.

By age 20, Olaf was a full fledged Viking and ravished the coastlands of England, Scotland, Ireland, Wales and France. On one of these excursions, he was wounded and requested baptism for himself and his warriors. Being zealous for his new faith, he became an eager "missionary." Wherever he went, clergy and teachers went with him.

After spending some time in Christian England, Olaf returned to Norway with a small fleet. He built a church on Moster Island, near Bergen. It's the earliest Christian site in the country. His terms to the pagan Norwegians were: "Be converted or die and have your homes burned!" This was the style of Christian kings in the Middle Ages. Pagan kings didn't give any choice.

In the Trondheim harbor, there is a small island called Munkholmen.

Olaf impaled the heads of the pagan rulers on its beach and warned that the same would happen to all if they were not baptized. They complied and elected him king in 996. Being a great grandson of King Harald Harfagre, they quite willingly followed him. Olaf founded Trondheim, called "Nidaros" in those days.

Olaf's undoing came when he proposed marriage to the widowed Queen Sigrid of Sweden, nicknamed the "haughty." They agreed on all the terms except one. She refused to accept his religion. Finally Olaf lost his patience and said, "Why should I care to have thee, an old faded woman, and a heathen bitch?" He angrily struck her in the face. (What a courtship!) Her parting words were, "This may well be thy death."

Sigrid had her revenge. She had Olaf ambushed at sea. Rather than become a prisoner and be tortured, he lifted his shield above his head and sank beneath the waves. He was only 32, but Norsemen still sing his praises. Olaf's statue stands atop a tall pillar in Trondheim's city square. I still feel Olaf's presence when I visit this ancient capital. There is a lesson in this story. The violence experienced by the boy, finds expression in the man.

CHAPTER 100

Celebration On
Moster Island

MOSTER IS JUST ONE OF 904 ISLANDS in the area called "Bomlo," located south of Bergen. It's a paradise for tourists, featuring boating, fishing and hiking. It's a place of magnificent beauty. We travelled through these waters in the summer of 1984.

Moster claims fame above the other islands as the place where Olaf Tryggvason landed at the port of Teigland in 995 with Viking warriors to begin his conquest of Norway. Here he held the first Christian worship in Norway. From there he sailed to Trondheim.

About 30 years later, in 1024, another Olaf (the "saint") visited the island to hold a constitutional convention for Norway. He wanted to make sure that the Christian faith was established in the land. The new law read: "The first commandment in our legislation is that we shall bow toward the east and pray to the Holy Christ for peace and a fruitful harvest and that we may keep our country settled and tilled and that our sovereign lord (King Olaf) may have strength and health; may he be our friend and we his friends, and may God be a friend to us all."

The church on Moster Island is the birthplace of the church of Norway. Olaf sent one of his clergy, Grimkell, whom he brought from England, to Bremen in Germany to receive consecration as bishop. He believed it would improve his political position if he was on closer terms with the authorities in Rome. The Bremen connection turned out to be useful. Adam, the archbishop of Bremen, was one of the best historians of the time. From him, we learn how both English and German missionaries worked together to make Norway Christian.

The church buildings used to be places of worship for the "glory of God," rather than for the edification of the worshippers. Instruction, sermons and fellowship, as we are accustomed to in America, were not a part of church life. The essential activities were done by the clergy with the people as spectators rather than as participants.

Christianity among the Norsemen was not a religion of love and compassion. Christ was seen as an heroic conqueror who saved the world when he, as "God Almighty," courageously mounted the cross in the sight of all men. It was courage and not compassion that won the Vikings to the new faith. The cross was seen as the ultimate sign of courage.

The people of Moster celebrate their heritage each year with a theatre production called "Kristkongane pa Moster" ("Christ the King at Moster"). The production is directed by Ragnhild Randal, whose husband, Haakon, was President of the Norwegian parliament and is now governor in Bergen. The Randals made a big hit with Americans in 1984 when they attended the Norsk Høstfest in Minot, North Dakota.

The play traces the history of the church from Olaf Tryggvason to Olaf Haraldsson. It tells how the people accepted the faith, then backslid and were finally won over permanently. The music used in the theatre can be traced to those original days. Instruments include medieval lyres, wooden shepherd's horns and trumpets made from goats horns. If you get to Bergen, try to get over to Moster.

You will also enjoy
reading these other
Scandinavian-interest
books
published by

The Scandinavian Spirit

By Arland O. Fiske

"The Scandinavian Spirit is a charming potpourri of anecdotes and observations about Scandinavians of every stripe — saints and scoundrels, kings and country folks, pirates and preachers. Fiske's subject is anything and everything that anyone with Danish, Swedish, Finnish, Norwegian or Icelandic blood has done or said that he thinks might be of interest to people today. He has an uncanny ability to ferret out interesting stories and little-known facts that most of us would never discover for ourselves, and his folksy, down-home style makes you feel as if you are listening to the tales grandpa used to tell. So fix yourself a cup of rich Scandinavian coffee, settle down in your favorite chair, and prepare to enjoy a smorgasbord of stories that will brighten your day and warm your heart."

Dr. William H. Halverson
Professor at Ohio State University (retired)

"For Scandophiles — and there are acres of this growing specie — good things come in groups of three and Arland Fiske's third book on our Scandinavian heritage is full of interest. In pleasant, painless prose, the info is nicely sectioned off, the amount of each being not too much, not too little, just right. 'Know ye the rock from which thou wert hewn,' exhorts the prophet Isaiah. The Fiske trilogy fulfills that obligation."

Dr. Art Lee
Author of *The Lutefisk Ghetto*
Professor of History, Bemidji State University

Well-known Scandinavian-American author and syndicated columnist Arland O. Fiske delights us, in his unique story-telling way, with stories and tales of Scandinavian people, places, history and traditions.

---

256 pages, 6"x9", softbound   No. HP-124 $9.95

The Scandinavian World

By Arland O. Fiske

CONTENTS

Well-known Scandinavian-American author and syndicated columnist Arland O. Fiske delights us, in his unique story-telling way, with stories and tales of the Scandinavian World.

The Scandinavian World

Arland O. Fiske

100 interestingly told stories about the people, places, traditions and history of Sweden, Norway, Iceland, Finland and Denmark.

Foreword by Alvin N. Rogness

248 pages, 6"x9", softbound   **No. HP-121**   **$9.95**

Skis Against The Atom

By Lt. Colonel Knut Haukelid

The outcome of World War II could very possibly have been much different if Knut Haukelid and his small, but courageous band of Norwegian soldiers had not been successful in sabotaging the Nazi's supply of "heavy water." The "heavy water" produced at a facility in occupied Norway was vital to Hitler's race with the United States to develop the atomic bomb. Knut Haukelid's "Skis Against The Atom" gives the reader an intimate account of the valiant and self-sacrificing service that the not-to-be-subdued Norwegians performed for the whole free world.

The exciting, first-hand account of heroism and daring sabotage during the Nazi occupation of Norway.

Excerpted from the Introduction of Skis Against The Atom by General Major Sir Collin Gubbins, CO of Special Operation Executive

I am glad to write for my friend Knut Haukelid an introduction to this enthralling story of high adventure on military duty so as to give the background to the operations which this book so vividly describes, and to show how they fitted into the wider picture of "Resistance." I hope, too, it will enable the reader to have a fuller appreciation and understanding of the remarkable exploits of a small and devoted group of Norwegian soldiers.

---

252 pages, 6"x9", softbound   No. HP-123 $9.95

Prairie Wind, Blow Me Back
By Evelyn Dale Iverson

Those who know the wind on the prairie know how capricious and powerful it can be. Yet men, lured by open land with rich black soil, bet against such odds that they could make a life for their families on this challenging frontier.

Prairie Wind, Blow Me Back

Evelyn Dale Iverson

Rakel: *"How can Renhild be so devious? I think she is the most evil person I have ever met!"*

"Nils thought of the prairie wind as a sparring partner. How could he beat this fellow?"

PRAIRIE WIND, BLOW ME BACK.

But where? It depends who and where you are.

For Nils, when he was homesick and struggling, it was his childhood home. But later it was other things.

For most of us, it is a glimpse of a different world a hundred years ago, and what life was like "in those days."

And like Nils, before we leave it, a look at desires, priorities, and values.

—*Evelyn Dale Iverson*

About The Author . . .

Evelyn Dale Iverson is a granddaughter of Nils A. Dale in this story, and a daughter of Hans M. Dale, the infant who came in a covered wagon to Dakota Territory over a hundred years ago.

The author is a native of Canton, SD, where her father was a professor and later the president of Augustana Academy. She graduated from Concordia College, Moorhead, MN, when her father was treasurer of that college. He also owned a part of the homestead in Miner County, which he felt close to, and his family visited often.

Almost all the names in this book are real places and real people, with the exception of Arne and Renhild, who are composites of others who lived "in those days."

---

158 pages, 6"x9", softbound   No. HP-122 $7.95